FREEDOM OF THE PRESS

William Ruckelshaus, *Moderator*
Antonin Scalia
Charles Seib
Edward J. Epstein
Floyd Abrams
Jack Nelson

WITHDRAWN

Elie Abel, *Moderator*
Kevin P. Phillips
Clay T. Whitehead
Ralph K. Winter, Jr.
William B. Monroe, Jr.

An AEI Round Table held on July 29 and 30, 1975
at the
National Press Club, Washington, D.C.

THIS PAMPHLET CONTAINS THE PROCEEDINGS OF
ONE OF A SERIES OF AEI ROUND TABLE DISCUSSIONS.
THE ROUND TABLE OFFERS A MEDIUM FOR
INFORMAL EXCHANGES OF IDEAS ON CURRENT POLICY PROBLEMS
OF NATIONAL AND INTERNATIONAL IMPORT.
AS PART OF AEI'S PROGRAM OF PROVIDING OPPORTUNITIES
FOR THE PRESENTATION OF COMPETING VIEWS,
IT SERVES TO ENHANCE THE PROSPECT
THAT DECISIONS WITHIN OUR DEMOCRACY WILL BE BASED
ON A MORE INFORMED PUBLIC OPINION.
AEI ROUND TABLES ARE ALSO AVAILABLE ON
AUDIO AND COLOR-VIDEO CASSETTES.

© 1976 BY AMERICAN ENTERPRISE INSTITUTE
FOR PUBLIC POLICY RESEARCH, WASHINGTON, D.C.
PERMISSION TO QUOTE FROM
OR REPRODUCE MATERIALS IN THIS PUBLICATION IS GRANTED
WHEN DUE ACKNOWLEDGMENT IS MADE.

ISBN 0-8447-2075-5
LIBRARY OF CONGRESS CATALOG CARD NO. 76-1468

PRINTED IN UNITED STATES OF AMERICA

CONTENTS

PART I

FIRST AMENDMENT PROTECTIONS

◈

William Ruckelshaus, *Moderator*
Antonin Scalia
Charles Seib
Edward J. Epstein
Floyd Abrams
Jack Nelson

WILLIAM RUCKELSHAUS, former deputy attorney general of the United States and Round Table moderator: The First Amendment to the United States Constitution states, "Congress shall make no law abridging freedom of the press." Throughout our history, the meaning of those words and the nature of the freedom they protect have caused controversy. Tonight, we're going to discuss with our distinguished panel, and later, the audience, three current controversies whose common theme is the tension between the First Amendment and the government's exercise of power through the judicial system.

First, newsman's privilege: Should a reporter, under any circumstances, be forced by the courts to reveal his confidential sources of information? In 1972, in the case of *Branzburg* v. *Hayes*, the Supreme Court said that under certain circumstances a newsman could be forced to testify before a grand jury and to disclose the identity of his confidential news sources. Since that time, and really before, several so-called shield laws have been introduced in Congress and in the state legislatures to protect the confidentiality of a newsman's source from judicial interference.

Second, libel: To what extent does, or should, the First Amendment to the Constitution protect the press from libel actions by private citizens who claim that they have been wronged? Is there, or should there be, a difference between the protection provided a private citizen and that provided a public figure?

3

Last, to what extent should the courts prohibit the publication of classified material? Starting with the *Pentagon Papers* case and continuing with the current sensational revelations about our intelligence-gathering agencies, a series of events has dramatized the question: should there be any limits stemming from national security needs on what may be published?

Let's start with newsman's privilege. Mr. Nelson, let me ask you: should the Congress of the United States pass a shield law absolutely protecting the right of a newsman not to reveal his confidential news sources anywhere in the country?

JACK NELSON, Washington bureau chief, *Los Angeles Times*: Yes, I think Congress should pass such a law and I think it should be an absolute law, an unqualified law. I would be opposed to a law that had qualifications and that might open such a bill to amendment in the future.

I'd like to say, by way of background, that I became a member of a group called the Reporters' Committee for Freedom of the Press, which was formed after Earl Caldwell was subpoenaed. He was the first of a series of reporters subpoenaed by the Justice Department during the Nixon administration. This committee of working reporters, mostly in Washington, saw that there was a necessity to protect reporters and their confidential sources, particularly in cases where investigation of government activities was concerned. From the outset the reporters' committee has favored an unqualified law.

Now, I think, for example, that if the Nixon administration had been able to subpoena Woodward and Bernstein of the *Washington Post* and other reporters, and had learned the identity of their confidential sources, Watergate would never have been uncovered. And there are many other stories that would never have come out if reporters could have been subpoenaed and forced to divulge confidential sources.

MR. RUCKELSHAUS: Mr. Scalia, you're from the Department of Justice. Do you have a contrary view or do you support Mr. Nelson?

4

ANTONIN SCALIA, assistant attorney general, Department of Justice: Well, I think Mr. Nelson's view is the most rational, next to what I think is the correct one, and that is that there should not be a newsman's privilege law. [Laughter.] The reason I say that his is the most logical position next to mine is that many people think that we should have a newsman's privilege law but that it should be qualified. And that, I think, would give us the worst of both worlds. The problem is, if you have a newsman's privilege law that's unqualified, you just can't live with it. And if you have one that's qualified, it just doesn't work. So, I think the best situation is the one that we now have, under which you cannot get a newsman to testify in court all the time—and there are judicial protections against harassment—but, on the other hand, in no instance can a newsman say categorically, "The law gives me an absolute privilege not to appear."

It really doesn't help to put the discussion in the context of the Nixon administration's subpoenaing of newsmen. It normally isn't the Nixon administration that subpoenas newsmen, it's normally a court in a criminal case. And as often as not, the newsman is subpoenaed not on behalf of the government, but on behalf of the defendant.

MR. NELSON: I would agree with you that the problem shouldn't necessarily be posed just in the context of the Nixon administration, but you've got to realize that the subpoenaing of reporters by the Justice Department did not begin until the Nixon administration.

MR. SCALIA: I doubt very much if that's true. I don't know all the facts on how many newsman's subpoenas there have been in the history of American jurisprudence. But I find it difficult to imagine that no newsman had ever been subpoenaed on behalf of either the government or the defense in any criminal trial prior to Nixon.

FLOYD ABRAMS, attorney for the *New York Times* and NBC: I can't give you an exact number, but we did look into this and it was certainly our impression, on reading every case we could find, that prior to the Nixon administration there had been very, very few cases of newsmen subpoenaed, certainly very few subpoenas issued by the Department of Justice, but that in the early days of that administration there was a new—and I think to the press and to the public—disastrous flow of subpoenas pouring out of the Department of Justice. Most of that, certainly, has stopped.

I'd like to add that we do have a qualified privilege now as a matter of law because of the decisions that have emerged. I would agree with Mr. Nelson that an absolute privilege would be a better idea. But I don't think we should let pass without comment the idea that a qualified privilege doesn't do any good. We do have one now. Case after case is coming down, in court after court around the country, establishing that in situations in which there are alternative sources for information, for example, you can't go to the newsmen first. And if you don't really need the information very much, you can't go to the newsmen first.

MR. SCALIA: I don't have a problem with that. The Justice Department guidelines for subpoenaing newsmen provide exactly that. I have no quarrel with that, if you're talking about a qualified privilege that is judicially created and administered or one that is administratively created and administered. But I thought we were talking about legislation that would establish a qualified privilege in the sense that it would not be adjudged on a case-by-case basis, but would be applied as a flat rule in a certain category of cases. I don't think that achieves the main purpose of the newsman's privilege law, which should be to open up confidential sources and prevent the so-called chilling effect upon confidential sources because—

MR. RUCKELSHAUS: Mr. Seib has a remark.

CHARLES SEIB, ombudsman, *Washington Post*: I just wondered if this was a realistic discussion. Is there any possibility at all of getting an absolute privilege law out of Congress?

MR. NELSON: No, I doubt seriously that there is any possibility. Now, at one time, there seemed to be a possibility.

MR. SEIB: Well, once you concede that you can't, wouldn't you rather stay with the First Amendment than get into a limited—

MR. NELSON: I would and I think you said you would, too—

MR. SCALIA: Yes I would, for two reasons: One is that the freedom of the press is a particularly important freedom under our Constitution and it has some special constitutional protection. And the second is that newsmen are particularly subject to harassment by subpoenas because they're in the business of finding out, of investigating facts. Police departments could come to rely upon them to do their jobs. For both of those reasons, I think it makes sense to accord newsmen some special protection through the courts and through the administrators—such as the Justice Department's not subpoenaing them willy-nilly, which we don't do. But beyond that, I don't think any more is needed or is, indeed, desirable.

MR. RUCKELSHAUS: Mr. Epstein, what's your view on the privilege?

EDWARD J. EPSTEIN, director, Twentieth Century Fund Project on News Agencies: To clarify the issue, I don't really think that to pretend that there has been freedom of the press up to the Nixon administration, and that somehow the Nixon administration violated this freedom of the press by subpoenaing reporters, is historically accurate. We had complete censorship in World War II and the Korean War when newspapers and magazines were told what to feature on their covers and what stories to publish, and editors were threatened by being drafted into the army unless they went along. We had the McCarthy period stretching into the early fifties, during which newsmen suddenly didn't have any sort of freedom to report what they wanted to. And while one might say that there were very few cases of the government's subpoenaing newsmen as witnesses before the Nixon administration, perhaps it didn't have to. But certainly in private libel

7

cases, hundreds of reporters were subpoenaed by one side or the other and made to divulge their sources.

You said at the beginning of the discussion that newsmen have a right and that the question is whether Congress should certify that right by law. But the Supreme Court has never found that a newsman has a right not to testify if he is a witness to a crime. The question really is this: is it worth elevating newsmen to some special status by giving them an absolute privilege which neither doctors nor lawyers have?

Mr. Nelson says Watergate would never have been revealed if newsmen could have been subpoenaed. I remember that Mr. Nelson made what I think was probably the single most important revelation on Watergate, as far as the public was concerned, when he published an interview with an ex-FBI agent, Alfred Baldwin, which detailed the entire Watergate crime, as seen by the man who was the intermediary between the Watergate burglars and the conspirators, Hunt and Liddy. Your paper published this entire interview, and if you had been subpoenaed—by the way, your editors were—and had gone to court and revealed that Baldwin was your source, I can't see that it would have made any difference.

MR. NELSON: That was a whole different story, though. Everybody knew Baldwin was the source. The point there was whether or not the tapes of the interview should have been turned over, because the interview had been conducted in confidence.

MR. EPSTEIN: But they were turned over. That's the reason that Baldwin—

MR. NELSON: Yes, but Baldwin wanted them turned over. Let me tell you, though, that I think that's a very interesting point. We were operating then in an atmosphere of government intimidation of the news media. For example, Ron Ostrow of the *Los Angeles Times* was with me on that case, and the two of us knew in our own minds that the government would try to get hold of the tapes of the Baldwin interview. We felt sure it would. So, when we came

8

back to Washington, we sent the tapes to Los Angeles, just in order to keep the government from getting them.

Now, what happened immediately thereafter was that Earl J. Silbert, the original prosecutor on the Watergate case, did tell me that the government was going to subpoena the tapes. He said, "What did you do with the tapes?" And I said, "Well, I can't tell you; you'll have to talk with our attorneys." And he said, "Well, we're going to subpoena those tapes, and if we don't, the defense will."

What happened was that the defense did subpoena them, and the Justice Department, in the person of Earl Silbert, stood up in court and said, "We have no objection to the subpoenaing of the tapes, and, as a matter of fact, we want to see them too." And that's exactly my point. There is intimidation, I think, of the media when the Justice Department is involved in the subpoenaing of reporters.

MR. EPSTEIN: But let's say hypothetically that aside from everything else, this witness, Alfred Baldwin, had already testified to the grand jury, and had told them the entire story he told you, so even if you had been intimidated to the point where you couldn't publish your story, still the grand jury would have heard the story and would have brought it out in the trial.

MR. NELSON: Well, no, that's not exactly right. Let's put it this way: in the process of our investigation—this was an interview that went on over two nights—we learned a lot of things that we did not print in the Baldwin story. It was a first person story by Baldwin; there were things that didn't go in because he could not substantiate them. We wanted to use these things as investigative leads. Do you know what happened? We sent the tapes to Los Angeles—the editors asked us to do that because we were afraid the government would get them—and we never got access to those tapes again, not to this day. And there was material on them that would have been helpful to us at that time in investigating Watergate.

MR. SCALIA: It was not the government which ultimately

subpoenaed them, though, was it? It was the defense in the case.

MR. NELSON: Well, it was the defense's subpoena, but it was the government that threatened to subpoena them. The government lawyers said, "If we don't subpoena them, the defense will." It was they who stood up in court and said, "This may raise a First Amendment question but, even if it does, the government has no objection to it."

MR. ABRAMS: I'd like to come back to something Mr. Epstein said earlier about how everyone has to testify to a crime that he's seen, which is certainly a true statement of the law. I don't think anyone who is advocating a news-man's privilege is really advocating that newsmen should be exempt from testifying about crimes which they have seen, except in one particular type of case which I could touch on. But what people are talking about—

MR. EPSTEIN: But isn't that what he means when he says absolute privilege?

MR. SCALIA: No, he doesn't. Mr. Nelson is talking about interviewing people.

MR. NELSON: I've never heard of a case—

MR. SCALIA: Most of the Justice Department subpoenas of newsmen involve two types of situations. One is the actual witnessing of a crime—for example, television news films of the shooting of George Wallace. And television, by the way, is one reason why the number of government subpoenas to newsmen has increased in recent years: television gives on-the-spot coverage of events at which unlawful action occurs or is charged to have occurred, such as demonstrations, Wounded Knee, and so forth. These are actual films of the alleged offense. Now, it seems to me that the government, which is trying to prove the offense, or even more so the defendant, who is trying to demonstrate that he didn't do what he is charged with, has an overpowering right to have that thing shown to the grand jury and then to the petit jury if the matter goes to trial.

MR. ABRAMS: That may be so in some cases. I think the problem with that is illustrated by the fact that ABC newsmen were stoned in New York City in the late sixties when they were thought of as police agents, an adjunct of the New York City police force, because they were being so routinely subpoenaed. The standard crime situation in which I think there is justification for non-testimony is the *Branzburg* case itself, where a reporter goes out, investigates, finds out that hashish is being made in Louisville, Kentucky, reports the story—which could not have been made known to the public without a pledge of confidentiality—and then is subpoenaed to testify and finally has to either leave the state or wind up in jail. I think the public is ill-served by that kind of law.

MR. SCALIA: That is not the typical case, and I don't think that any discussion of absolute newsman's privilege should center solely upon the government's desire to get evidence (as opposed to the defendant's) or solely upon the confidential source cases, which are the most appealing from the standpoint of the newsmen. Most cases do not involve confidential sources.

The second very common type of situation, besides news films of events, involves tapes and kidnap letters and such things mailed to newspapers or television news stations or radio stations after a kidnapping—ransom notes, or notes threatening that such and such a building is going to be blown up. Now, on occasion, these have been denied, when the police wanted them for the purpose of trying to detect where the individuals concerned were located. I see no reason for the extension of a privilege in such cases. There's no confidentiality involved whatever.

MR. RUCKELSHAUS: Have you ever been chilled by a government subpoena?

MR. SEIB: When I was managing editor at the *Washington Star*, we had the Agnew incident in which there was some effort to get our reporter's notes. That died. Otherwise, I haven't.

But I was wondering—we talk about the increase in

the number of subpoenas and legal efforts to get material from the press. Is any of that due to the increased separation between the press and the authorities in the government? Maybe things that used to be done cooperatively between the press and the authorities are now done at arm's length. Maybe the distance between the two has widened, because we're more conscious now of the need for separation. Is this one of the factors here?

MR. SCALIA: You gentlemen would know better than I.

MR. NELSON: I wouldn't think so. I mean, it may be a minor factor, but I wouldn't think so. For example, newspaper reporters are cooperating all the time in cases involving congressional investigations, in cases involving Justice Department or police investigations. It's not unusual for a reporter to learn of some information that had to do with a crime and to cooperate with law enforcement officers. I don't know of any cases where reporters really witnessed crimes—except, as you say, the case where they asked somebody to let them see him make hashish so that they could do a documentary on it, in which case, nobody would have known that the crime had taken place if the documentary hadn't been made.

You cited a hypothetical situation when you were testifying on the Hill about the shield law. And you said that if there were an absolute shield law, the situation would be such that a television station could have an interview with Patty Hearst, and then the Justice Department or other law enforcement officials would be unable to compel the television station to say where it had found Patty Hearst, and so forth. Well, the point is that a lot more would be known about Patty Hearst after an interview like that than had been known before, a lot more than would have been known if the interview hadn't taken place. And had Patty Hearst known that this television station would tell the Justice Department or anybody else where she was, she would never have shown up for the interview. This happens all the time.

MR. SCALIA: Well, the point I was making at that stage

in my testimony was quite different from the one we have just been discussing. I think that situation could occur if there were an absolute shield law. And the main reason I think that situation would be bad is that a society could not really take the battle against crime seriously if it could allow such an interview to happen. I don't know where Patty Hearst is on the FBI's most-wanted list, but let's assume she's number one. And there she is, big as life on the screen, in living color, with a news reporter having an interview with her. I just don't think a society can take its law enforcement efforts seriously if it can allow something like that to occur.

MR. ABRAMS: That is the case in twenty-four states where there are privilege laws, many of which are absolute. In New York, for example, if that interview had occurred with Patty Hearst, the New York state authorities would not have been able to require a newsman to disclose his source.

MR. RUCKELSHAUS: I think Mr. Scalia is saying he doesn't agree with those things.

MR. ABRAMS: I think I understand that, but what I'm saying is that the country hasn't exactly collapsed either. New York may not be precisely the best example of anything these days. [Laughter.] But we do have these statutes around the country. Yet I can't cite any examples of horrors, and none has been cited in testimony that I've read— even yours.

MR. SCALIA: Well, maybe New York doesn't have Patty Hearst. I don't know. I think—

MR. ABRAMS: New York has Abbie Hoffman.

MR. SCALIA: —if Patty Hearst offered an interview, somebody would snap it up mighty fast. And I think that something like that would have an enormously corrosive effect upon effective law enforcement; that the entire society's respect for—

13

MR. NELSON: Wouldn't the FBI and the Justice Department know a lot more about Patty Hearst if they saw her interviewed on television than they know right now? I mean, they know very little now.

MR. SCALIA: No, not necessarily. I guess they'd have a current photograph of her; that might be helpful.

MR. EPSTEIN: But she might be disguised.

MR. SCALIA: You're seriously asserting that this would be a help to law enforcement efforts?

MR. NELSON: Well, I don't know, but it wouldn't be a hindrance.

MR. ABRAMS: I would seriously assert that it would be more useful to the public to be able to watch an interview with Patty Hearst than not. And the effect of what you're saying is that, in the future, at least, the public wouldn't be able to watch such an interview.

MR. SCALIA: Well, what if it were Jack the Ripper? Would that make any difference? There would be Jack the Ripper in living color, saying: "Hi, out there. I'm being interviewed on television. I know the police can't get this film and can't find out where I'm being interviewed, because the laws we live under say it's more important to watch me than it is to catch me." [Laughter.]

MR. NELSON: Suppose it were Adolf Hitler when he was alive.

MR. EPSTEIN: You talk about a person being compelled to testify if he witnesses a crime—what would happen if you or another reporter that you respected interviewed someone who said, in the course of the interview, or inferred, that he might assassinate the President—

MR. NELSON: Well, obviously, I'd go directly to the authorities.

MR. EPSTEIN: No, but let's say this came out in the interview, that you put it in your story, and that then your notes were subpoenaed by the authorities to see if they could build a case against the person who had made the suspicious statements. Would you submit your notes? Would you testify only about the portions of the interview that contained the threat? Because this was the *Caldwell* case.

MR. NELSON: In what way is that the *Caldwell* case? That's not the *Caldwell* case at all.

MR. RUCKELSHAUS: Let's not argue about that. Let's take it as a hypothetical situation. What would you do?

MR. NELSON: I'd go directly to the authorities—if somebody told me he was getting ready to assassinate the president or anybody else. And that's the reason I say this is a false issue. I don't think any reporter who's a human being would listen to someone threaten, or say they were going to kill, someone else—no matter who it was—and not take action.

MR. SCALIA: What is a reporter?

MR. NELSON: I define a reporter as anybody who's gathering the news for public consumption. And that's the reason I think the unqualified shield law would not just apply to me, but it would apply to anybody who went down to city hall, got information from a confidential source, came out, and distributed it. I think there ought to be an unqualified shield law.

MR. ABRAMS: I think we have to decide which examples are more real, since the resolution of these questions has got to depend largely on that. You do have a nice case, I think, on the presidential assassin, in the abstract, and on Jack the Ripper, in the abstract. But I think that there's a more real case, and that reality is Paul Branzburg. That reality is also a reporter who goes down to a police station, interviews a policeman, and is then made to testify about his own interview with the policeman. I have just been through that with a reporter from the *New York Times*—

made a witness to his own interview with a policeman, some of which was confidential, some of which was not. In totality, treating reporters this way can only interfere with the public's getting the kind of information it should get. I really don't think that the assassination example—which lawyers, incidentally, are confronted with in court every time they argue these cases—

MR. SCALIA: Was that the prosecution or the defense seeking the reporter's testimony?

MR. ABRAMS: In that case, it was the defense.

MR. SCALIA: It often is. And if I were the defendant, I wouldn't feel so horrified—in this instance, maybe—about not giving the newsman as much leeway as he would like. It's a very hard case, when you're talking about whether or not to send a man to jail.

MR. ABRAMS: Yes, but that doesn't place any First Amendment input on the scale at all. Sure it's a hard case. There are a lot of hard cases. And the fact that a defendant wanted the reporter's testimony does dispose me more favorably toward the subpoena than a similar subpoena from the prosecution would. But it doesn't seem to me that that answers the question.

MR. SCALIA: No, it doesn't answer it. And I concede that in each case in which a subpoena is being sought the court should ask, "Is this really necessary to the case? Is it being done for the purpose of harassment?" and so forth and so on. But that is quite different from laying out either a categorical shield law or even a qualified law that gives an absolute privilege in certain defined cases—which I find very difficult to define.

MR. RUCKELSHAUS: Do you think, Mr. Abrams, that there is a right to know on the part of the public?

MR. ABRAMS: Let me say that that is a phrase that troubles me because if there is a right to know, then I suppose the public has a right to compel the press to print things or the judiciary may have the right or someone may have the right to decide what it is the public should know. I think that the First Amendment ultimately serves the public by letting it learn things—letting it hear things and letting it see things on television—that it wouldn't otherwise know.

There was a case out in Indiana last year in which ABC was barred by a prior restraint, a court injunction, for over 200 days from doing a show demonstrating, proving, that plastic cribs burned more quickly than wooden cribs. I think the public had a right to know precisely what ABC wanted to tell them, and that the injunction was a most offensive interference with the public's right and the press's right.

MR. RUCKELSHAUS: What about the case of the producer of hashish and the impact that the interview with him might have not only on the public but on the children of people watching that television program? Does the society have some very strong interest in revealing who is producing that hashish and is likely to introduce it into the market?

MR. NELSON: That was not the thrust of that particular program, though, was it?

MR. ABRAMS: In the *Branzburg* case, the thrust of the story was how easy it was to make hashish in Louisville.

MR. NELSON: Yes. It was *not* to show people how to do it or to encourage its use.

MR. RUCKELSHAUS: It showed somebody making hashish, though, who would then, presumably, distribute it in the community.

MR. NELSON: That's right. But the point of the program, though, was not to promote the use of hashish, but to discourage it. That was the point of the program, was it not?

MR. SCALIA: Yes. That gets us back to my Patty Hearst case. I don't like that kind of show because in effect it is telling the society: "Look what people can get away with. We can go in and take a picture of this thing." The viewer thinks: "Why don't the cops use this evidence to get those guys that are making the dope? We know the dope is going to go out on the streets." But, no, we can't do anything about it.

MR. ABRAMS: I know you don't like that kind of show—

MR. SCALIA: I think it's outrageous, and it has to corrode the whole attitude of the society towards crime.

MR. ABRAMS: I really think that the Department of Justice and the courts should refrain very strongly from imposing what they like and don't like—which is what you're talking about—upon the law. It may be—and, indeed, it is—true that a lot of things the press prints are destructive and harmful to people. I think we've made a decision in the First Amendment to run that risk, and not to run the risk of having government officials decide what is harmful and what is not.

MR. RUCKELSHAUS: How great should that risk be? Let's move on now to the issue of libel laws. Should any right accrue to a private citizen to sue the press if it steps over certain bounds in accusing him of a wrong?

MR. NELSON: Well, private citizens have that right, don't they? They have the right under libel laws.

MR. RUCKELSHAUS: Yes, they do. I wonder whether you agree that they should.

MR. NELSON: Well, under my theory of absolute privilege, I'm not so sure that I'm too much in favor of libel laws, I have to admit. But citizens do have the right to sue.

MR. RUCKELSHAUS: Unfortunately?

MR. NELSON: Yes, unfortunately. You know—I'm almost in favor of absolute and complete press freedom, whatever that may be.

MR. EPSTEIN: Then it raises the issue of whether the public would get the truth or the lie. If reporters had the right to publish anything and to conceal their sources—so that they could even manufacture a source if they wanted—it's not clear that there would be any way of testing the truth of what they were publishing or that, in the long run, newspapers would have any credibility. It's impossible—

MR. NELSON: Well, newspapers are part of a free enterprise system, and they sink or swim eventually on their credibility.

MR. EPSTEIN: But the newspapers that succeed with the public might succeed because they publish very plausible lies or unbelievable truths.

MR. NELSON: Some of them do.

MR. EPSTEIN: Right, and that's what you would want to see?

MR. NELSON: That's not what I want to see; it's what happens in this free market, in this market of free ideas. And I don't regard it as all bad. It's not all good, but it's not all bad either.

MR. EPSTEIN: There's an alternative—

MR. NELSON: Yes, I think the alternative is government regulation.

MR. EPSTEIN: No, the alternative is to have strong libel laws—

MR. NELSON: Well, that's government regulation.

MR. EPSTEIN: —to have the kind of libel laws for the press that we have in book publishing or in the academic field.

MR. NELSON: You're in favor of stronger libel laws than we now have?

MR. EPSTEIN: The libel laws we now have are a joke when it comes to public figures. It's almost impossible for a public figure to sue successfully. This is very convenient for me, as a journalist—I mean, it makes things very easy. But I think that what is going to happen in the long run is that the press is going to lose its credibility, because so many things will be published that no one will know what to believe.

MR. NELSON: Mr. Seib here, as ombudsman for the *Washington Post,* is part of the effort to help us restore that credibility.

MR. RUCKELSHAUS: What does ombudsman mean, Mr. Seib? I think it is a growing trend.

MR. SEIB: It is a growing trend. The press is trying to police itself. I don't know if the effort is going to work or not. I've been in this job eight months now, and I'm not sure whether I'm doing good or harm.

But until the press is ready to accept its responsibilities a little better than it has, than it does generally, I think that probably the libel laws, at least the laws protecting the rights of the private citizen who doesn't expose himself by running for office or by taking public office, are the minimum we should have. I can't quite see that the press is yet ready to have all restraints removed so that it relies totally on the marketplace and the ultimate triumph of good over evil to solve the problem. The area that I am most concerned with—fairness and accuracy and balance—doesn't really come under the libel laws. The libel laws are sort of a last resort, and, as you say, the public figure really doesn't have much access to them any more.

MR. NELSON: Well, you're the access.

MR. SEIB: I'm the access now, to the extent that a corrective piece or a discussion piece ever catches up with the original error.

MR. RUCKELSHAUS: Let me try to return later, Mr. Seib, to this question of what might be done by the press itself to ensure responsibility—because I think it's important. Do you accept any other restrictions—for instance, perhaps those advanced in the name of national security—on the right of the press to print material that comes into its hands?

MR. SEIB: I'm sure one could concoct a case where national security or the security of certain individuals made restraint in publishing a story necessary, at least for a short time. But, generally speaking, the claims of national security, I think, should be very harshly examined by the editors and by the press. My position is that the press does have absolute privilege under the First Amendment.

MR. EPSTEIN: Absolute privilege to do what?

MR. SEIB: To report whatever it gets hold of.

MR. RUCKELSHAUS: The courts, in other words, have no role in trying to prevent the press from printing a story— even if it were to involve what would be, by a reasonable man's definition, a grossly irresponsible act, perhaps might even jeopardize lives. Even in that case the courts would have no right to move in?

MR. SEIB: Well, that's hard to say.

MR. RUCKELSHAUS: How about in practice?

MR. SEIB: In practice, first of all, I think the courts would move in.

MR. NELSON: Look, it's not very hard to get the press not to run a story.

MR. SEIB: That's right. It's too easy, as a matter of fact.

MR. NELSON: Yes. For example, take the case of William Colby who went around and got the *Los Angeles Times* and the *New York Times* and the *Washington Post* and

Newsweek and *Time* and NBC and CBS and ABC and Public Broadcasting, and I don't know who else, not to run the Glomar Explorer story on the grounds of national security. Now, the story ran, and nobody's been able to tell anyone how national security was really involved in that.

MR. SEIB: The picture of that official running around town, trying to stop the story, dribbling little bits of information as he went, because he had to divulge a little more information in each conversation in order to convince the parties not to publish—that picture is really ridiculous.

MR. EPSTEIN: But do you think that the public interest was served? Actually, by the way, I think I read the story in the *Los Angeles Times.* Didn't they publish it two weeks before—

MR. SEIB: They had the wrong ocean. [Laughter.]

MR. NELSON: Well, that was before Mr. Colby had—

MR. EPSTEIN: The story was already published. But, aside from that, I don't see what public interest was served by publishing that the CIA was perfectly legitimately retrieving a Russian submarine from international waters, and the government officials never heard of such a—

MR. NELSON: Let me ask you something. Here was a ship out in the middle of the ocean, operated by Howard Hughes, who's always been—

MR. EPSTEIN: It wasn't operated by Howard Hughes.

MR. NELSON: Well, all right. It was owned by Howard Hughes. It was a Howard Hughes operation. It was a Howard Hughes-CIA operation. Sure it was. The CIA itself says it was.

MR. EPSTEIN: It was a CIA operation.

MR. NELSON: It was a Howard Hughes-CIA operation. In any event, do you see nothing wrong with a private contractor out on the high seas recovering a Russian submarine, and with the involvement of Howard Hughes—who's always been sort of on the fringes of shady government operations? You see nothing wrong with that? And you don't think the American people are entitled to know about that?

MR. EPSTEIN: Wait a moment. The retrieval of the submarine was done by Glomar. Howard Hughes built the ship, but then it was taken over by another company, Glomar—

MR. NELSON: Yes, which is also a Howard Hughes operation.

MR. EPSTEIN: Well, in any case, I think it was—

MR. SCALIA: Listen, I'll say no to his question, if nobody else will. I don't see anything wrong with it. I think it was a great job, if indeed it happened the way they said it did.

MR. RUCKELSHAUS: Well, why not publish it?

MR. EPSTEIN: The reason not to publish it is very clear: it might have stopped them from retrieving the rest of the submarine.

MR. ABRAMS: That's what they say.

MR. EPSTEIN: And publishing the story destroyed the expenditures—

MR. NELSON: Do you think that the Russians didn't know the ship was out there? The CIA said they assumed that the Russians knew.

MR. EPSTEIN: But the key issue is who is to be the arbiter of what gets printed.

MR. NELSON: I would say the press.

MR. EPSTEIN: You want the press to be the arbiter. Let's say that a piece of information bears on national security. You believe that the press would somehow know what the Russians knew and what the Russians didn't know?

MR. NELSON: The same national security argument was used to cover up Watergate, to cover up the Ellsberg burglary. National security was stamped on almost every one of the revelations that came out after Watergate.

MR. EPSTEIN: In other words, you want to be the arbiter of whether some operation is a national security matter or not? Let's just get this very clear.

MR. NELSON: Well, let's face it, yes, I think the press should be—

MR. EPSTEIN: And you feel that your education and your knowledge of the world qualifies you to decide—

MR. NELSON: Not just me—the press generally.

MR. EPSTEIN: Well, I just couldn't take that responsibility.

MR. ABRAMS: The alternative, Mr. Epstein, is to allow the Department of Justice and the court system, that other branch of government, to make those same decisions as to what the press can print. And I think that that involves very considerable risks which were well recognized in the First Amendment itself. The *Pentagon Papers*, of course, is a good example of that. God knows we heard enough about national security in that case, about documents which were historical in nature—

MR. NELSON: But that was another case where the press cooperated with the government: it did not run those papers.

MR. SCALIA: Who do you mean by the press? I asked before how you would decide who was a newsman for this purpose, and now you're talking about the press in general.

Some of the cases that have come before the courts have involved reporters from an SDS underground newspaper. Do these people have any less claim to being reporters than those from, say, the *New York Times*?

MR. NELSON: No.

MR. SCALIA: All right, then you say it's one thing if a spy gets information and disseminates it, but it's quite another if he's working on the staff of the *Daily Worker*. Is that the distinction you draw?

MR. ABRAMS: If it's the *Daily Worker*, it may be espionage and if it's espionage, it should be liable to criminal prosecution. But if it's news gathering—I think there is a distinction. [Laughter.] I don't think it's a hard distinction.

MR. SCALIA: I wouldn't want to be on the other side in court, having to demonstrate that distinction.

MR. ABRAMS: Well, I would hope that you would recognize that distinction between the *Daily Worker* and other newspapers which gather news for the purpose of reporting it to the public.

MR. SCALIA: Well, you surely can't distinguish between one newspaper and another. You must distinguish on the basis of some principle as to how news is acquired or why it's acquired.

MR. NELSON: Look, you know that if a reporter for the *Daily Worker* is involved in espionage work, the results are not going to show up in the *Daily Worker*. [Laughter.]

MR. SCALIA: So whether it's published or not is the criterion?

MR. ABRAMS: The way the law decides things like this is on the basis of intent and on the basis of a variety of other factors which would, in fact, distinguish spies from newspaper men. Now, I think that you are right in saying that there are some hard issues as to who is a journalist and how far the protection ought to go. And I think that that's a legitimate area—

MR. SCALIA: They are very hard issues. In fact, I know of no way that you could prevent defense secrets from being released—and solicited, I suppose—by someone so long as he's willing to print them in the *Daily Worker*, and I'm not entirely willing to—

MR. ABRAMS: But the fact is that we have lived in this country for over a hundred and fifty years now, and that's not exactly the danger that has dominated our history. The danger I detect arises from a government which seems to continually lie to the public, rather than from a press which doesn't even do enough to gather the facts the public ought to know. Now, that is a matter of judgment you may not agree with; I think you will not. But it does make a difference as to what you think about that subject. We've just been through years of that kind of lying based on claims of "national security."

MR. RUCKELSHAUS: Mr. Abrams, does the fact that the term national security has been abused in the past—and I think that most people would agree there's been some abuse—mean that, therefore, it has no validity whatsoever as a justification for preventing the publication of material?

MR. ABRAMS: No, I don't think so. So far as I'm concerned, I agree with what Justice Stewart said in the *Pentagon Papers* case—that the only time that you can enjoin a newspaper from publishing information is when publication will surely result in direct and immediate and irreparable harm to the public. Now, that's very hard to prove, but it's supposed to be very hard to prove.

MR. SCALIA: I don't insist on going much further than that. I thought you were taking a categorical position that—

MR. SEIB: Well, who decides it?

MR. SCALIA: Who decides everything? The courts decide. [Laughter.]

MR. SEIB: We haven't spoken about the price here. You have to assume that to have a free press—and I'm convinced that our system of government wouldn't work without it—there's a price. Now, perhaps it would have been better if we hadn't printed the Glomar story. Then the CIA might have been able to go back and get the code machine, if there was one. But that was the price we pay for a free society.

MR. EPSTEIN: But what have we gained for that price, other than one day—

MR. NELSON: I don't know that we've lost anything.

MR. EPSTEIN: I don't know that we've lost anything either but—

MR. NELSON: You see, we don't even know if we got anything. We know what the CIA officials told us, and that's all. And we do know they don't always tell us the truth.

MR. EPSTEIN: But that's my problem. I have no way of knowing what a code machine is, much less how it would be valuable in figuring out some Soviet codes or not figuring them out. I agree with you; I'm absolutely ignorant in this field. But then how can I, a newsman, be the arbiter of whether something is legitimate national security or not? That's the dilemma, as I see it.

MR. ABRAMS: The solution to your dilemma is that, given a credible government, maybe the press ought to sometimes believe it.

MR. EPSTEIN: Yes.

MR. ABRAMS: I have no objection to Mr. Colby going around Washington trying to persuade people, but I think the press ought to make the decision whether or not to believe him.

MR. NELSON: Obviously, a lot of editors did believe him, because they didn't run the story until finally Jack Anderson broke it on radio one night. So, obviously, a lot of editors and a lot of television news executives did believe Mr. Colby.

MR. SCALIA: Well, I think that this analysis of the possible harm the Glomar thing could have done is really not as profound as it ought to be. What action the Russians can take if they already know about the U.S. attempt to retrieve the submarine may be quite different from what action the Russians can take and feel obliged to take if they already know it and the whole world knows that they know it. Did it not dawn upon newsmen that this might make a difference?

MR. SEIB: I think that it might make a difference, and that gets back to the price. Do we want our press to conduct itself on the basis of how its actions are going to influence Russian reaction or foreign policy or the day-to-day saving face or not saving face with another country?

MR. RUCKELSHAUS: How high does the price have to be, Mr. Seib? Supposing a story really would jeopardize the lives of several people, or even one person, and it could be demonstrated pretty carefully that it could. Do you still leave it up to the press as to whether or not they publish information?

MR. NELSON: Can't you give us an example yourself? Can you give us the one you gave us earlier, the one that occurred when you were in the FBI?

MR. RUCKELSHAUS: Well, I could give an example of the press responding positively to the—

MR. NELSON: But it's a very interesting example, and I think it goes to the heart of what we're talking about.

MR. RUCKELSHAUS: It does. Both the *Washington Post* and the *New York Times*, when I was the head of the FBI, responded affirmatively in the sense that they didn't publish information which the FBI indicated would jeopardize the life of an agent. They restrained themselves from doing so. On the other hand, under your theory of the courts not being able to interfere, in the event a less responsible press than the *New York Times* or *Washington Post* decided to go ahead and publish, the FBI would have been helpless.

MR. NELSON: Suppose they had decided to go ahead and publish. Would you have gone to the courts to try to enjoin them?

MR. RUCKELSHAUS: I think if I were convinced in my own mind that this would jeopardize the life of an individual agent, yes. On the other hand, I'm the moderator and take no position on—[Laughter.]

MR. SEIB: In the discussions with the papers about the FBI man, did the question of timing come up? Did they say, "Well, get that man out of there because the—"

MR. RUCKELSHAUS: As a matter of fact, the papers entered into the conspiracy with a lot more alacrity than I did, Mr. Seib. They were willing to go around the government and concoct a giant scheme to keep it from being published, but I was very uncomfortable participating in that.

MR. ABRAMS: That's because you're so credible. [Laughter.]

MR. SEIB: One of the sidelights of the Glomar story is that a lot of the papers that agreed to suppress it really didn't have much in the first place. They were just as happy to suppress. [Laughter.]

MR. RUCKELSHAUS: We're about running out of time. Let me get back to the theme that you touched on, Mr.

Seib, and that your job as ombudsman certainly touches on. There obviously are some instances where an individual, particularly a public figure, can be harmed by a newspaper story. The courts have traditionally refused to intervene or interject themselves between the publication and the harm that might be done to that individual. What can the press itself do about irresponsible stories about things that are not related to that individual's responsibilities but nevertheless may be harmful?

MR. SEIB: Well, I think the press can try to correct it.

MR. RUCKELSHAUS: Or is this just a price we have to pay?

MR. SEIB: Well it's a price, all right; the mistake is the price we pay, but that doesn't say that the mistake can't be rectified in some manner. The press, I think, is very slowly becoming comfortable with the idea of correcting a mistake.

I was recently involved with a mistake concerning George Wallace—and not in my wildest dreams had I thought I would end up as the defender of George Wallace. But I wasn't really defending him. Rather, I was defending the reader's right to have a fair report on what Wallace had said, and I think that is what the press has to worry about. When you're dealing with a public figure—someone who's running for office, is a possible candidate, or whatever—it isn't the harm you do to him that counts so much —for he can usually handle that—but rather what you do to the reader's right to the truth. And, in the case in point, what the *Post* wrote about Wallace certainly didn't harm him and, in fact, it probably increased his support in some sections.

MR. RUCKELSHAUS: On that note of the press helping George Wallace, let's move on to the second half of the program. We now turn to members of the audience for questions and comments.

HOWARD PENNIMAN, Georgetown University: I would like to ask a question directed in part to Mr. Scalia and in part to the two members of the press who are present. I am concerned about the degree to which the press considers itself responsible for the accuracy of a story and for rectifying any errors which may be involved.

If I may, just one moment, supply the context in which this might be answered. Back in June (1975), the *Los Angeles Times* printed a story by George MacArthur about heavy U.S. bombing of South Vietnam in the last days of the war. Then Mr. Seib wrote an excellent commentary on it a little later. Then last week, on July 25, the *Los Angeles Times* published a retraction of it—written, indeed, by George MacArthur himself. The *Post*, on the following day, printed a note on the retraction. In printing the note, the *Post* said it was clear that the White House and the Pentagon had not been responsible for any significant bombing. What the *Post* did not include—but the *Los Angeles Times* did—was that all of the efforts made by the reporter in Washington could find no evidence of any significant bombing, in fact, having been ordered by anyone.

Which still leaves some questions: How far did the *Los Angeles Times* go, or should it have gone, in protecting something which you more or less laughingly refer to as American face-saving—which is involved in this? Is it enough to simply absolve the President? Is it enough to simply say, "Yes, we have now stated there was not significant bombing"? That still implies that there was some type of bombing, a fact which has not yet been demonstrated.

31

And all of this from one of the wonderful sources which we are to protect.

I would like to hear from Mr. Scalia on whether he believes these newspapers gave adequate protection to national security and whether their judgments appear to be good, and to hear from either of the others on how such actions might be defended.

MR. SCALIA: I don't want to answer that question—I guess, for the reason that I really jump off the boat as far as the proper role of government is concerned when it comes to correcting the news media, being sure that they are reporting accurately and correctly. Correcting the news media is none of my business and I don't think it is any of the government's business.

That matter is quite different from what we were talking about earlier—that is, the simple questions of whether the government can obtain the information that is necessary for the administration of justice and whether it can, in some situations at least, prevent the dissemination of information that would be detrimental to vital national interests. These two questions are quite different from the problem of the irresponsibility of the press—if you want to call it that. I think we have made a decision in the First Amendment that the press can be as irresponsible in what it chooses to say as it wishes and that the corrective is the voice of those who are responsible—as well as, to some extent, the libel laws, I suppose.

MR. NELSON: I would agree with Mr. Scalia—that it is not something for the government, or anyone other than the newspaper itself, to take action on. Now, as to the case you refer to, the government did take action, in that it not only denied the story, but pursued its denial. As a matter of fact, I happened to run into Ron Nessen, the President's press secretary, at a bar on an evening before the retraction came out. It was not just the day before but some time before. Nessen told me, "We called in, and we told the *Los Angeles Times* that the White House unequivocally denied that the bombing had taken place. Yet you ran the story, and down in the story you ran the denial parenthetically." He said, "We think that's wrong." I replied, "Well, I don't know any more about it than what you've just told me and what I have seen in the paper, and if we don't have more to substantiate it than that, I think you are right; I think it is wrong."

He said he was going to write to the editor, which I'm sure he did. And Charles Seib did write an editorial column on it, as the ombudsman for the *Washington Post*, in which he said the *Los Angeles Times* had never been able to substantiate its original story. Bill Thomas, the *Los Angeles Times* editor, took it very seriously and looked into it. George MacArthur, who had written the story and was in our Saigon bureau, came back to the United States and spent two or three weeks trying to prove whether the information was wrong or whether it was right and the government's denial was wrong. He could never really get any substantiation for the story, so he admitted it and wrote the retraction.

I think the point is—and Bill Thomas said this is the article that MacArthur wrote—that the *Los Angeles Times* was wrong: it should not have run a story that had been unequivocally denied by the White House; it should have gone back to MacArthur. And this is not an excuse but it is what happened: the communication never got back to MacArthur that there was an absolute unequivocal denial and the story ran with the denial.

Bill Thomas says the paper should never have run it. We ran a page one correction which Charles Seib said was probably the longest retraction in the history of journalism. The *Washington Post* ran it on page one and the *New York Times* picked it up and ran it. I think we should have run it. I don't know what else you can do beyond that, but I think it is a good reflection of how newspapers are now trying to be responsible on these things. We've got an ombudsman now, for example, or at least a media critic, by the name of David Shaw. He does the same sort of criticism, in a sense, that Charles Seib does and he frequently writes a story that we run on page one. He has criticized the *Los Angeles Times* as well as other parts of the news media when he has found that they've been in error.

I don't know what else a newspaper can do when such an error occurs other than correct it. If a reporter got too far out and was involved in the story, I suppose he might run the risk of his job. I'm sure that whoever was on the desk and failed to get the message of the White House denial back to MacArthur has probably heard from the editor about it. I don't know what else you can do.

MR. SEIB: I would like to comment on that because I think that that whole episode raises a couple of points that go far beyond the story. First of all, one of the main reasons I wrote the column was not that I knew the story was right or wrong, because I didn't at that time, but that I had a feeling that neither the *Post* nor the *Times* was ever going to tell us whether it was right or wrong. I think the press has been very reluctant to clean up its own messes. Both the *Post* and the *Times* led with that story that Sunday morning, making a charge, and then sticking a couple of parenthetical denials in it. I knew it was going to just die there unless somebody gave them a push. And I am satisfied myself that there would not have been a follow-up unless somebody had.

The second point the incident illustrated to me was the credibility problem the government now has. When the President's press secretary and the secretary of defense's press secretary deny, not in a pro forma way but in the most unequivocal terms possible, that an event occurred, and when all that happens is that the story is run exactly as it was originally written with two little parenthetical paragraphs stuck in to show how fair the press is—I just think that is a rather significant commentary. And I also think it is a commentary on the press for MacArthur or the *Los Angeles Times* to say, "Well, gee, if we had known they really meant the denials, we wouldn't have done it that way." I mean, what are these guys supposed to do?

MR. NELSON: Well, you understand the message never got to MacArthur, however, from the foreign desk. That was part of the problem.

MR. SEIB: Should he have gotten it?

MR. NELSON: It should have gotten to him—there is no question about that.

MR. SEIB: Well, but I am raising the question of whether it should have and whether that mattered.

MR. NELSON: I think it does matter. I mean, as we know, there were all sorts of denials during the Nixon administration and a lot of them were not equivocal denials.

MR. SEIB: That's what we are dealing with now.

MR. EPSTEIN: You say you don't know what the press could do about publishing something that might be a falsehood. Now, I think there is a very simple thing the press could do and it doesn't involve the government at all. The journalist could simply publish his source. In this case, if MacArthur had published the name of the person who had told him that the United States had bombed Vietnam on that day, that source could have been quickly discredited. Let me give you an example: the charge was made that Alex Butterfield was a CIA agent in the White House. To its credit, the *New York Times*, while it didn't name its source, intimated so strongly that its source was this man Fletcher Prouty—was that his name?—

MR. ABRAMS: Yes.

MR. EPSTEIN: —that very quickly people zeroed in on Prouty, who then named his source as E. Howard Hunt. And very quickly E. Howard Hunt then denied that he knew anything at all about Butterfield, and Butterfield was cleared without a major calamity.

MR. NELSON: George MacArthur would have no sources if he identified them. You must understand that.

MR. EPSTEIN: Well—but is it better that the public have the truth? Who is the client of the newspapers? Is it the public or is it the source? If you are trying to protect the source or the reporter, sure it is better for the reporter if he never names his source, but what about the 10 million readers of the *Los Angeles Times* who read that—

MR. NELSON: They now know the story was wrong. What else can one do?

MR. EPSTEIN: They might not. The same people who read the story on one day might not have read it on another day. Also, the *Los Angeles Times* denial wasn't unequivocal. It said that "no significant bombing" could be established. It becomes much more confusing. I think the public has a right to know where the information comes from, even at the risk of a reporter's losing his source. In a case where there is a denial by the Department of Defense, the reporter should be forced to name his source.

MR. NELSON: You really would dry up sources. There is no question about it.

MR. EPSTEIN: Why not dry up sources?

MR. NELSON: That's what we live by. The only way we get information out of the government is to have confidential sources—let's face it.

MR. EPSTEIN: I agree that we might earn less of a living and it would be a harder living, but I think—

MR. NELSON: I'm not talking about our living.

MR. RUCKELSHAUS: Let us have some more participation by the audience.

FIELDING McGEE, Reporters' Committee for Freedom of the Press: I have a question for Mr. Scalia. The Justice Department guidelines were formulated to establish standards—among other things, as you mentioned earlier—so that the press could not be harassed. And yet, according to the Justice Department's own admission, in late April, upwards of 20 percent of the subpoenas issued to newsmen by the Justice Department, which would have been about 25 out of 125, were not even signed by the attorney general before they were issued. And yet, that is a specific provision of the attorney general's guidelines. I am just wondering how you can reconcile your statement that there is administrative or judicial protection when in fact the guidelines are being violated?

MR. SCALIA: That has nothing to do with judicial protection, of course; you would still be accorded the judicial protection when the subpoena was sought, regardless of what antecedent procedures the Justice Department had used.

What we are talking about, for the benefit of the audience who may not know, are procedures whereby the Justice Department will not even seek a subpoena from a court (and the court has the discretion to deny it even when it is sought) without following established criteria which include a personal ruling by the attorney general on each subpoena. Now, you are calling attention to the fact that in some of these cases—I don't recall whether your figures are correct, so I'll say a large number of individual cases—preliminary consent to the subpoenas was not sought from the attorney general. As soon as the department found out that that was the case, the subpoenas were quashed and, in some cases, reapplied for after the attorney general's approval. In other cases, they were simply washed out.

The Justice Department's guidelines include, in addition to personal approval by the attorney general, such things as the following: The approval will not be given unless—except in exigent circumstances—the information sought from a newsman is merely to confirm information that has already been derived from some other source; he will not be used as a new investigative source, in other words. Second, a subpoena will not be sought unless negotiations have been conducted with a newsman to try to come to some accommodation whereby the needed information would be provided, and so forth. I think the significant feature of the application of these guidelines is that in the twenty-six months preceding the report to the Congress that you spoke of, there had been only thirteen instances in which reporters had been subpoenaed against their will.

I'd like to add a comment that I meant to make earlier: I think there is developing within the news community—and I regret its development—a morality that proscribes providing information to the law enforcement authorities except under subpoena. So a large number of the subpoenas issued from the Justice Department are voluntary subpoenas in the sense that the newsman has said, "Sure, I agree this is information the police ought to have but I don't want to turn it over; it violates my code. Get me a subpoena." There were only thirteen instances where that was not the case, and only one instance in that period of twenty-six months in which the Justice Department involuntarily subpoenaed a newsman to obtain information from a confidential source. One case in twenty-six months! I think that is tremendously impressive evidence of the restraint that has been exercised at least at the federal level.

Now, to give the other side its due, most of the criticism of the behavior of the law enforcement authorities towards the media has been directed not at the federal level but at the state law enforcement authorities. And I have no idea how many states adopt similar procedures.

REED IRVINE, chairman, Accuracy in Media: I would like to direct my question to Mr. Abrams. Mr. Abrams, we have one ombudsman on the stand and there is another ombudsman with the *Los Angeles Times*. I think one of the most serious problems that they are confronted with involves the electronic media where the problem of getting corrections on the air, on television and radio, is much more difficult than in the press. Yet, over 60 percent of the people today are getting their news primarily from television. I would like to have your comment on the institution of ombudsman as a corrective to error and a factor promoting fairness, and to know whether you would recommend this type of institution for the company you work for as a lawyer, NBC.

MR. ABRAMS: I have followed with interest, Mr. Irvine,

your interest in this subject and particularly with respect to NBC. I suppose I am obliged to say now, speaking for myself, that it seems to me an ombudsman is one tool which some newspapers have found to be useful in doing what they can to make sure that when errors have been made, stories get corrected. There are other ways.

I don't think that you and I should go on about our litigation which has involved the very matter which you raised, but certainly having an ombudsman is one way that newspapers have sometimes found to be useful. Another way, certainly, is for broadcasters and newsmen to make sure that, when mistakes are pointed out to them, the mistakes are double-checked. Whether the check is made by an ombudsman or by the other regular procedures of a network is not as important as ensuring that it is made.

NBC, to my knowledge, makes those checks. I think networks, as a whole, are becoming increasingly attuned to the need for making checks as speedily as possible and for making sure that if there are any reported or alleged inaccuracies, they are corrected. I have some personal regrets that television does not contain more of the equivalent of a letters-to-the-editor page. I think, for myself, that that would be a useful thing for the networks to have. Sometimes they have its equivalent. NBC has had some programs of this type, and so have the other networks. NBC now has a "correction page" at the end of its news broadcasts. All of these are different ways, I think, to respond to the feeling on the part of some that television has not been responsive enough in this area. I do think there has been very substantial progress and I hope it will continue.

I. WILLIAM HILL, *Editor and Publisher* magazine: I would like to know how many members of the panel—I wish you would poll them—favor an absolute shield law; how many are for the shield law and how many are willing to depend on the First Amendment? Then, as a second part of my question, I'd like to know whether they think any sort of shield law could get through Congress.

MR. RUCKELSHAUS: Well, as long as you don't make me respond by holding my hand up on any of those, I'll be glad to poll the panel. I think we could put Mr. Nelson on the side of an absolute shield law. I don't know about Mr. Abrams and Mr. Seib. Where would you fit?

MR. SEIB: Well, I'd stick with the First Amendment, partly because I think that is philosophically and logically the way to go and, secondarily, because I don't think an absolute shield law could be passed, and anything less than that would open the door to more problems than we have now.

MR. ABRAMS: I'm afraid I just haven't decided and no one has ever asked me before. I really don't know. I am well aware, I think, of the arguments on both sides. Certainly if judicial decisions were more hostile to the press than they have been in recent years, I would, with no difficulty at all, come out for a shield law even if it were a somewhat qualified one. If I had to vote on it or advocate a position on it, given the development of a useful qualified shield, which I believe now exists because of the First Amendment itself, I just don't know where I'd come in.

MR. RUCKELSHAUS: Mr. Scalia, I think, has made his position clear, in favor of the First Amendment.

MR. SCALIA: Yes, and the reason is that a qualified shield law just doesn't do any good. If its basic purpose is to protect a confidential source and render him willing to talk, you hardly go up to a confidential source and say, "Now, I won't tell this to anybody unless . . ." and then detail the exception. He is not going to care; you either have to tell him "Nobody will get this," or else leave it to the First Amendment. And I think most people believe you should leave it to the First Amendment.

And on the gentleman's second question, it is my impression from the members of Congress that I speak to, both those in favor of and those opposed to the shield law concept, that the likelihood of any legislation this time around is somewhat less than it was the last time around.

MR. RUCKELSHAUS: Mr. Epstein?

MR. EPSTEIN: Well, from the point of view of personal convenience, I would like an absolute shield against anyone asking me any questions about anything I didn't want to refer to, including the IRS examining my expense voucher. But from the point of view of what would benefit journalism most, I don't think that absolute privilege is either workable or necessarily good. I think that the more journalists are able to conceal their sources, the less likelihood there will be of general credibility in the press.

Obviously, journalists have to be protected against harassment by malicious subpoenas. I am not sure the distance between myself and Mr. Nelson on this point is so great. Most of the things he considers to be outrageous I find outrageous, too. But I think that the First Amendment could provide a great deal of protection, especially with guidelines from the government, so I would not be for the shield law. I also don't think it would be passed.

ALAN EMORY, *Watertown Times*: I would like to take this discussion one step further and ask Jack Nelson a question. Given the fact that courts and judges change, just as Mr. Ruckelshaus can testify that justice departments change, how do you square your preference for total freedom of the press with support for even a totally unqualified shield law, since a shield law by its own definition is an invasion of the First Amendment and opens the door to further changes in the First Amendment?

MR. NELSON: Well, I don't think that it does open the door to change. I think it would if it were a qualified law. But if it were an absolute, unqualified shield law, it would only really be a congressional sanction of what I think we already have, and that's the First Amendment privilege. I do agree that if a shield law were qualified in any way, it would be worse than no shield law at all. And I also agree that there is no chance, at least now, to pass an unqualified shield law; even members of the news media differ greatly among themselves on this matter.

41

MR. SEIB: Even if you got an absolute shield law and put it on the books, wouldn't it open the door to second thoughts by Congress? I mean, isn't it easier then to move in on the First Amendment than if you didn't have that shield law?

MR. NELSON: Well, there is that argument and a lot of people have made it. I don't happen to believe it.

MR. ABRAMS: I think if one could trust the courts a little more, one would be less disturbed—at least I would—by the idea of federal shield legislation. That is to say, there is no logical reason why the adoption of more protection for the press need lead to any less protection for the press if Congress repealed it next year. There is a considerable body of First Amendment protection now which, in my view, is well established in the law. If Congress provides more, it ought to be able to do it in language clear enough to say that we are not undercutting the First Amendment.

MR. NELSON: Incidentally, wasn't it made clear in the *Branzburg* decision by Justice White that if Congress so desired, it could pass a shield law?

MR. ABRAMS: Yes, it was made clear in the decision that Congress could pass a shield law and that the state legislatures could pass shield laws. For the interest of the audience, it is worth mentioning that in two state court decisions in the last year or so, state court judges have expressed considerable qualms as to the constitutionality of the state shield laws, one in California and one in New York, on the ground that the shield laws interfere with the inherent power of the judiciary to run its courtrooms. I think those decisions are wrong and, in my view, flatly inconsistent with the *Branzburg* case, but they are there.

JACK MASON, attorney: Mr. Scalia, I am interested in the fact that the Justice Department has promulgated these guidelines, which I gather do not have the force of regulation or statute. Specifically, I'm interested in the way these things happen within the Justice Department, undoubtedly without any kind of public discussion or chance for the usual hearings. Yet they constitute the de facto policy of the Justice Department presumably across the country. Is there any thought to bringing those guidelines to the level of regulation or even statute? You have stated that you are opposed to any substantive shield law, but at least these guidelines, if they were promulgated as regulations, would give the newsman, I suppose, some threshold procedural protection against harassment. Guidelines have a way of being sloughed off when the heat gets turned on.

MR. SCALIA: Your point is well taken, at least with respect to some types of guidelines which do disappear rather easily. These, for some reason shrouded in the mist of prehistory—which means before I got to the Justice Department—were not issued as regulations but they are published in the Code of Federal Regulations. They are publicly well known, and the department does feel itself bound by them.

As I say, where these guidelines have been violated, the department has consistently withdrawn its subpoenas. I personally do not see any problem with issuing them as regulations. On the other hand, I don't see any great necessity to do so either. They are published in the Code of Federal Regulations; they are publicly known; they are consistently abided by; and in cases where they aren't— and this is one point that hasn't come up in today's discussion—of all the interests in society, the press is probably the most capable of making its complaints known. So I don't think that these guidelines will just drop out of existence.

MR. NELSON: That's a good point, but also we, the press, are always out there where everybody can see us, too. All of our mistakes are out there. I want to say that I think there has been an awful lot of concentration here on mistakes and inaccuracies within the media. And my own observation, as a reporter for an awfully long time, is that—particularly in the larger papers, most professional papers and the networks—there are relatively few substantial errors. And when big mistakes are made, as in the bombing story, I think normally some corrective measures are taken—if not in a retraction, in an editorial page piece or something. I think there is a great deal of dwelling on inaccuracies in the media.

MR. RUCKELSHAUS: Seventy-five percent of the time, you are accurate?

MR. NELSON: I think that the news media, generally, and I really mean this, are accurate on substantive matters an extremely large percentage of the time. There are an awful lot of words in a daily newspaper; you are bound to have some inaccuracies. But I think relatively few substantial errors are made.

MANNY KAY, National Newspaper Association: My question is for Mr. Scalia. If the Justice Department has had only one occasion in the last twenty-six months to subpoena the name of a confidential source, why is it fighting so hard for a tool so susceptible to grave abuse?

MR. SCALIA: Because, for all I know, that one case might have involved a prosecution which would not otherwise have been established, taking off the streets somebody who might have caused great harm to another person, having already caused it to one. Even more important, in that one case or in another case like it, it might be the defendant who could have been wrongfully convicted of a crime had he not been able to find out from a newsman some confidential information that would enable him to demonstrate his innocence. I just don't see why, given the ability to place reasonable restrictions upon use of the power, the power should be entirely eliminated.

MR. ABRAMS: I think it should be said that we do have a number of state cases in which reporters have gone to jail and that the subject that we are talking about tonight is thus not entirely an abstract one. A California reporter was jailed for over fifty days; other reporters have gone to jail in New Jersey and elsewhere for refusing to divulge their confidential sources. One can argue, as we have, about the degree of protection that ought to be afforded in this area, but it is not an abstract problem.

MR. MASON: I would like to ask Mr. Abrams with respect to the last two questions whether you, as an attorney, would like to have some procedural protections, if you defended a newsman from subpoena in court, similar to those, for example, attendant to the application of a wiretap, so that you not only could defend the newsman from having to answer the question, but even before you got there, you could point to something more than rather ephemeral guidelines in the Justice Department? Would you like to have regulations or statutes to give you that kind of procedural ammunition?

MR. ABRAMS: How can I say no to a question like that?

MR. SCALIA: I resent the description "ephemeral." The guidelines are there in black and white. They are published in the Code of Federal Regulations and lawyers have used them in court.

MR. ABRAMS: There is, first of all, what I consider still an open question as to the degree to which the Department of Justice is bound to follow those guidelines as a matter of law and whether, if it does not follow them, a subpoena will be quashed by the court for that reason alone. Let me add that the kind of qualms that I have about a newsman's privilege statute are the kind that are commonly voiced: that when Congress starts down the road who knows what it will do next year, that a newsman's privilege statute might be taken by the courts to detract from the First Amendment protection which already exists, and so on.

The kind of procedural protections which your question speaks to seem very different to me. I think it would be useful to have procedural protections which would require a prosecutor and courts in advance to give a kind of notice and to follow specified methods, instead of the rather willy-nilly issuing—in my experience this happens in state courts in particular—of subpoenas from prosecutors and from defense counsel.

I should say also that, while my instincts are such that I think the courts ought to be especially careful in a case in which a defendant has subpoenaed a reporter, that is not and should not be the end of the inquiry either. There are many instances, to my personal knowledge, in which reporters are subpoenaed by defense counsel who are lazy, who just don't go out and do their work or who think that since the reporter has gone to the scene, surely he must have something somewhere which bears upon the subject. Apart from the interference with confidentiality, which is sometimes involved, meeting this demand is in fact an immense burden upon the press and particularly the smaller press—not the large institutions we have been referring to today, which, I am happy to say, can afford lawyers and the like.

Smaller newspapers in small communities around the country have again and again been subjected to procedures where they had to bring reporters to court, wait in court for days to give testimony which is ephemeral and which is of no real relevance to the case. I think some kind of procedural mechanisms would be of very great use.

RICHARD McCORMACK, American Enterprise Institute: I understand that the British take a somewhat stricter attitude toward the press than we do in this country and I would be very interested in any comment you people might have on the Official Secrets Act in Britain and the British libel laws, whatever harm they cause and whatever good they bring.

MR. ABRAMS: I'm very interested in that subject, particularly because a leading case is going on in Great Britain right now involving Mr. Crossman, the former cabinet member who wrote diaries contemporaneously with his service in the cabinet about the internal workings and deliberations of the cabinet. An effort is being made now in the English courts to prevent that type of material from being published.

It's a very different system from ours which would even take seriously, as the English certainly do, that application to the court. There is no statute which authorizes prevention of publication in the Crossman case because the Official Secrets Act does not apply. Nonetheless, they are still going to court seeking a prior restraint barring the press's right to publish. Under the Official Secrets Act, of course, the *Pentagon Papers* could not have been published. Indeed, much that was published about Watergate could not have been published because claims were made of national security in the Watergate case itself.

I think that we are well served by a strict reading of a First Amendment that accepts many of the risks that many of you—Mr. Epstein, certainly—have pointed out tonight. In return for accepting those risks, we get a press which is free enough to be, in the language of the Supreme Court, robust and uninhibited. And I think that we are all better served by it.

I have no particular comments on the British libel laws except to say that they are, of course, far stricter than our laws. Some English editors and publishers have gone to jail for things which would not even state a cause of action under American law. Again, I think we are well served by having a press which does not have to withstand that sort of regulation, although one has to recognize that we, as a society, consequently risk having the press print things which are offensive to many.

CRAIG MOORE, law student, University of Virginia: I would like to address my question to Mr. Nelson. Given that there are certain precepts underlying the allocation of decision-making authority in society, and given that certain tensions are bound to arise between, on the one hand, the public's right to know and, on the other hand, the public's right to be protected in certain instances depending on certain circumstances, what particularly qualifies individual newsmen as opposed to either the Congress or the courts to decide whether or not information should be divulged in the service of either of those entities?

MR. NELSON: Well, I think the First Amendment gives us the right to make that decision. And I would say this in answer to the question about Great Britain: we know a lot more about what goes on in our government than they know in Great Britain, and I think that's good. There are very few things that go on in government that should be secret and I see nothing wrong with you or any other citizen making the decision as to which they are. It is just that I think the First Amendment covers it.

MR. IRVINE: President Truman said he didn't think the government could operate on the presumption that everybody had the right to know everything. And he also said that he didn't see much difference in the results if official secrets were published in the newspaper or if they were transmitted to the enemy by microdot or secret radio.

I think Mr. Abrams has suggested that intent was the key factor and I would like to ask perhaps Mr. Abrams or Mr. Nelson whether the results are not the important factor. It really doesn't make any difference whether the transmission was by the *New York Times* or the *Washington Post* or the secret radio code or—

MR. ABRAMS: I will try first, Mr. Irvine. Intent was one of the factors I mentioned which is relevant to the decision as to whether someone has violated a criminal law. I think it should be. As far as I'm concerned, we simply have to recognize that there is going to be much that is published in a free press which either the government or some of us will think is harmful to the national interest in some fashion.

For example, in the *Pentagon Papers* case, the government made much of the fact that it would be embarrassing in terms of our relations with certain foreign governments to have some of the material in the *Pentagon Papers* published. I think one may take that as true, *arguendo*—I must say I have some doubts about it—but suppose that the government's claim were valid? What I am saying is that even if it were valid, that is a price we should be prepared to pay. Now if your question about that, for example, were "Is it a real price?" my answer would be yes. That's where I think the First Amendment came out, and, I think, wisely.

The First Amendment aside, in terms of the imposition of criminal sanctions, it is factors such as intent which make the difference. It should make a difference if somebody publishes information about Glomar which he thinks, regardless of whether all of us agree, the public ought to have or if someone transmits the same information to the Russians on a secret basis with the intent to harm the United States. Is the effect the same? In a sense, it is. Sure, *in a sense*, it is. The Russians get the information either way. Yet it seems to me that the law should continue to make the distinction that I've indicated it does.

MR. SEIB: Of course, the difference is that if the Russians get the information from the press, then the government, the press, and everybody knows that they have it, whereas if they get it from a spy, obviously, everybody doesn't know.

MR. EPSTEIN: So it is worse to get it from the press.

MR. SEIB: Why is that?

MR. EPSTEIN: Because then they are forced to take action because they know everyone knows.

MR. SEIB: Well, that gets a little—

MR. SCALIA: That's true, you know. The Gary Powers spy plane incident was an example of that phenomenon. We have reason to believe that the Russians knew that these U-2s were overflying their territory and had known it for a long time, but as soon as it became a matter of public knowledge, highly visible action on their part was necessary.

MR. SEIB: Which do you think is a healthier situation?

MR. SCALIA: If I were going to write an article about that, I wouldn't pick that example; I would pick another one. I only used that to make the point that it does make a difference. It is not always better if everybody knows about a situation; sometimes it's worse.

MR. SEIB: All right.

MR. RUCKELSHAUS: Let me ask you, Mr. Nelson: you indicate that the responsibility to act responsibly should be left primarily, if not exclusively, to the press. What effect do you think the competition for news has on the exercise of this responsibility?

MR. NELSON: Well, I think it has a tremendous effect. And not only that, I think the whole diversification of the media has a tremendous effect.

MR. RUCKELSHAUS: Positive or negative?

MR. NELSON: A positive effect. I don't think there is any question about that. If the press goes way out on a limb on something, as we did on the Vietnam bombing, we are going to get caught short on it. With all the news magazines, the networks, the large newspapers, all of the wire services, AP, UP, and the supplemental news services, if a news report really contains a substantial error on a matter of some importance, the public will know about it instantly. And it would know about it even without Mr. Seib's work because other publications would find out about it, and the newspaper that has been shown to be in error can't retain its credibility.

MR. RUCKELSHAUS: How often do other publications point out the errors on—

MR. NELSON: On matters of substance? I think they do it frequently. They may not say that a specific report was in error, but they print the story as it really happened.

MR. RUCKELSHAUS: To what extent do you think the competition that occurs forces you to come out with stories before you are able to completely verify their accuracy?

MR. NELSON: That does happen sometimes and it is regrettable, but it doesn't happen very often. I can remember a few very bad examples. I can remember, for example, the Eagleton matter involving Jack Anderson, which I thought was bad and which he later admitted was bad. But how many instances can you think of on a really major matter where a newspaper or radio or television came out with something of real importance that was wrong because it was trying to be first? When a paper does it, it is inexcusable.

MR. RUCKELSHAUS: Let me tell you of one—the Agnew case involving the vice president of the United States. The competition among reporters was fierce in that case; they were all over the Justice Department and the U.S. attorney's office in Baltimore, plus the vice president's office itself, trying to get information on an ongoing investigation for which there was no cover-up. Many of the stories—

MR. NELSON: All of it happening, however, in the aftermath of Watergate when people would have been expecting a cover-up.

MR. RUCKELSHAUS: I am not saying it wasn't understandable, but that doesn't make it justifiable.

MR. NELSON: It doesn't. I agree with you.

MR. RUCKELSHAUS: Many of the stories that were published were full of inaccuracies.

MR. SEIB: Don't you think the Butterfield-Prouty incident might not have happened if NBC and CBS hadn't been so competitive?

MR. NELSON: I think it is possible. And I admit that there are cases of competition prompting papers to print stories they're not absolutely sure about, but I don't think there are that many major cases. When it does happen, it is absolutely inexcusable. There is no way to justify it when newspapers or television end up reporting inaccuracies because they're so eager to be first. I don't think that is the trend, either. It seems to me the trend is in the opposite direction. I know it is the trend, for example, on the *Los Angeles Times,* and has been for a long time. I've had particular cases in the past few years where I would be on a story and, let's say the *New York Times* would be working on it, the *Washington Post* would be after it, and my editor would say, "Just hold on, don't release the story now; be sure you get it all and be sure it is absolutely right. We don't care if they're first." Now, everybody wants to be first, of course—there is no question about that. But I think the trend in journalism in this country is to be right.

MR. RUCKELSHAUS: "Don't get it right, get it written," is no longer screamed from the city desk?

MR. NELSON: I think that is right.

MR. SCALIA: Mr. Ruckelshaus is not suggesting, I take it, that we'd be better off if we had only one newspaper.

MR. RUCKELSHAUS: No, I'm not, but I think the point that is often missed by the public is that the competition for news, particularly here in Washington, is very strong. This competition has a way of creating its own momentum that pushes a story into print before there is adequate opportunity to verify it.

　　I was in the middle of the Agnew investigation, and I thought that was a prime example. Why, the *New York Times* would editorialize about the Justice Department's leaking information which we were unable to find, saying, "Why don't they protect this poor man's rights?" And then it would unleash a horde of reporters to find out the leaked information. There were certain olympian—

MR. ABRAMS: Wasn't that the *Washington Post*?

MR. RUCKELSHAUS: No, it was the *New York Times*.

MR. NELSON: Don't you agree, though, that there have been unusual times in Washington in the past few years, with Watergate and the resistance of government to giving out information of legitimate public interest, information that should have been given out? It took eighteen months to find out who was on the White House payroll during the Nixon administration. I mean, just matters you could go down to City Hall—

MR. RUCKELSHAUS: I'll bet you still haven't found out.

MR. NELSON: That's right.

MR. RUCKELSHAUS: I think that we are running out of time. In closing, I would like to indicate my appreciation and that of the panel for the audience's participation. By no means will we all leave in complete agreement. But the principle that has been defended here with such great articulateness is precisely our right to meet as free men and women and discuss, freely and with little chance of interference, issues as important as freedom of the press and the future of this society. So let me thank all of you for your participation and thank the members of the panel as well for being here. [Applause.]

PART II

REGULATION
OF THE MEDIA

Elie Abel, *Moderator*
Kevin P. Phillips
Clay T. Whitehead
Ralph K. Winter, Jr.
William B. Monroe, Jr.

ELIE ABEL, Dean, Columbia University Graduate School of Journalism and Round Table moderator: Our topic for discussion tonight—Freedom of the Press, Regulation of the Media—is a topic that agitates a great many Americans in our time, particularly when they think of the broadcast media, television and radio. The key questions are these: Are the broadcast media too powerful? If it is true, as we are told, that broadcast journalism has become the preeminent source of information for the American people about the state of the nation and the state of the world, then the question arises, should the government not be more vigilant about what goes on the air and who puts it there? Do we need more regulation or less? Or should we be regulating in a different way? Does the First Amendment, which guarantees freedom of the press, apply to journalism on the air as well, or only to the printed word? And if it does apply to broadcasting, how do we justify any federal regulation at all, in view of the explicit injunction in the First Amendment that Congress shall make no law abridging freedom of the press? These are serious questions. And among our panel members today are men of strong views on these very questions. You will be hearing from them in a moment.

Consider, for example, the question of access to the media. Who is entitled to reach that enormous national audience? We have heard in recent days about the case of Jack Anderson, a well-known Washington correspondent who recently taped a television interview with President Ford, an interview which the three commercial networks, he tells us, refused to broadcast because it was not the product of their own staffs. Or take the earlier case of Frank Mankiewicz and his associates who went to Cuba and taped an interview with Fidel Castro. A portion of that interview did, in the end, appear on the CBS network, but only after Mankiewicz had returned to Havana with Dan Rather for a second interview which bore the imprimatur of CBS. If men as prominent and as experienced as Mankiewicz and Anderson can't get air time on the networks, what hope is there that the views of comparatively anonymous Americans are being heard and will be heard?

Also to be considered is the question of media concentration. Here in Washington, for example, we have two major newspapers at this time—and it is possible that there may be only one before long. There is a much larger number of broadcast outlets in this area. Yet the broadcasters are regulated on the theory of spectrum scarcity and the newspapers are not. Is this good public policy?

These are questions that have been raised by people of various political convictions. I have been impressed by what seems to me a reversal of roles on some of these questions between liberals and conservatives. The liberals of ten or fifteen years ago, as I recall their views, were all in favor of the fairness doctrine and a more assertive regulatory role for government. Today liberals are among those who cry out for the removal of the fairness doctrine. Conservatives, on the other hand, who have traditionally abhorred government intervention and undue regulation, seem now to be calling for more regulation.

I would like to explore some of these ideas with my fellow panelists this evening. Let me begin with my old friend and former colleague, Bill Monroe. Bill has made a kind of off-hours career of studying the fairness doctrine, the First Amendment, and their application to broadcast journalism. What about that, Bill, do you have any doubt that the First Amendment does, and should, protect the broadcast media, and where does that bring you out when it comes to regulation?

BILL MONROE, NBC News: I think the First Amendment should protect broadcasting, but I don't think it does. Some years ago as a young man I worked for a newspaper. I was very impressed with the spirit of independence on the part of the editors of the newspapers. They didn't care if something they put in the paper offended a major political figure. Later I went to a television station and slowly I discovered that the managers of the television station were a little afraid of government. They were timid, conscious of government looking over their shoulder in a way that the newspaper publisher and editor for whom I had worked had not been. I began to feel that I was in a medium that was a little bit less than free, and it worried me.

I think we have gotten into this position because radio and television came along only about fifty years ago, and because initially they did not appear to be important news media. They looked more like entertainment devices. And we developed a regulatory apparatus—based on the necessity to allocate channels—that was not originally intended to get into control of content, but which has gotten into control of content, partly accidentally, because we didn't realize what we were doing, and partly because control of the content of any medium often serves the purposes of politicians.

The politicians would very much like to get some leverage over the print media if they could, because they can make it easier for themselves by writing their own rules as to how journalists cover politics. They are trying to do this, and to some extent they have done it for the broadcast media.

So I think the whole regulatory apparatus—for example, the fairness doctrine—has produced broadcast media that are less adventurous than they could be and don't have the full courage of the print media. We can get away from this if we realize what's happening and move in the direction of less regulation. We should throw out the fairness doctrine, throw out the so-called equal time rules for coverage of political campaigns—which, among other things, have deprived the American people of debates such as they had between Kennedy and Nixon back in 1960—and abolish most of the Federal Communications Commission, the parts that apply to program content of broadcasting in particular.

MR. ABEL: Kevin, what do you think about all of that?

KEVIN P. PHILLIPS, author and syndicated columnist: Well, I tend to react somewhat cynically to people talking about the poor media, saying that they are under the thumb of the politicians, because I think we have seen in the last couple of years that, if anything, it tends to be a little more the other way.

I have seen polls—I think that *U.S. News & World Report* in the last two years has asked opinion leaders in the United States to rank the power centers in this country in order of their importance. In 1974 the television networks were ranked ahead of the White House, and in 1975 it was virtually neck and neck. Just two months ago or so, John Connally spoke about how the network newscasters, the anchormen, had more power than the speaker of the House of Representatives, more power than the majority leader of the Senate and the minority leaders of both houses. These are several measures of what we are up against. We are not up against a purely commercial situation. I think it's a question of power, power that is responsive to nobody.

Perhaps the people from the networks will say, "Yes, Walter Cronkite wouldn't be there unless everybody liked him." But in point of fact, the viewers only get to choose among three T.V. newscasters. It's not as if they are choosing among "X" number of politicians. So I think the power that the television networks have is quite out of keeping with the situation that applies to individual newspapers, although, of course, you can argue that some of the major newspapers and media conglomerates have the same amount of power.

But I think we are dealing with something like the runaway power of Wall Street in the 1920s before it was regulated, of the railroads in the 1880s before they were regulated. And I think we need something that either forces the networks to open up access, or breaks up the networks into smaller units that would be more responsive to the average American's opinion and less arrogant than those we see at the present time.

MR. ABEL: Kevin, that's a view that I have heard from the other end of the political spectrum. It surprises me a little bit to have it coming from you, a conservative. But on this matter of how much power the broadcasters actually possess, define that a little bit more, if you can. Where does the power reside? What is it that the broadcasters do that gives them this power?

MR. PHILLIPS: I would say that the principal power with which I would be concerned, and which I have seen a lot of conservatives express concern over, really resides with the networks as opposed to the individual television stations. After all, the stations are subjected to a regulatory process, but the networks are not. Here are these three operations that have this incredible power to beam into our living rooms the political agenda for the nation; they choose the people who say in the morning or the evening who is good and who is bad, what happened in the world, what you are to think about, what the agenda is. To me it is not the individual stations in Albuquerque, Dover, Delaware, or wherever that have too much power. It is the networks. The people who are not responsible are those who sit up in New York behind whole corridors of power, ten to twelve offices removed from any place the public could possibly penetrate without an official pass, just like the Pentagon. These are the people that are calling the shots. Now, I think that's what public policy has to reach toward.

RALPH K. WINTER, Yale Law School: I'm having trouble understanding why it follows from the supposed great power of the networks—and I'm skeptical of the assertion that any one institution has that much power over us— why it follows from that that there has to be some kind of control over the content of television programs. Indeed, I go so far as to say it most certainly does not follow from that. I can't imagine a better way to centralize control in one body than to say the government ought to regulate program content. Then you can be sure that the broadcast media will, indeed, have power and it will be exercised with a deliberation and an intent that may well be lacking in the present situation.

Let me put a proposal to you. Suppose that we were to make the television stations, the broadcast media, like the newspapers, open to competition from weekly news magazines, other newspapers, monthly magazines, and the like. Suppose we were to abolish the FCC, have the government define frequencies so that chaos would not result from everyone trying to broadcast on the same frequency, put all the frequencies and the channels up for bid, let them be sold, and then let the property rights in these frequencies be reflected on pieces of paper, freely transferable among people. Would not that take care of all of your objections?

MR. PHILLIPS: I think it would take care of some of them. Actually, I merely indicated support for the fairness doctrine at the present time, as opposed to favoring the approach of controlling program content. I think a very effective application of economics to break up the concentration, or to open it up, would be a preferable alternative. Now, I'm not sure whether precisely what you have outlined is the answer, but I think it's a movement in the right direction.

MR. WINTER: Indeed, I think that the media are in great peril today, not because there is or was an administration that was out to get the media, but because the dominant themes in American political life are bound to be turned against the media. You are, I think, most adroit in picking up these themes and articulating them. You have picked up the Galbraith-Nader theme of the manipulation of people by the media because of the power that advertising has, so that people have to be protected. You have picked up the theme of economic concentration, which Mr. Galbraith and Mr. Nader use. And, indeed, you even picked up Mr. Gardner's theme of the influence of wealth on the political process. And I think you have shown how these dominant themes in American life will inevitably be turned from the auto industry to television. It just follows as night follows day—although, let me say in your defense, that I regard you as a true son of the Harvard Law School. [Laughter.]

MR. PHILLIPS: I know what that means, coming from a Yale man.

CLAY T. WHITEHEAD, former director, U.S. Office of Telecommunications Policy: Well, I think we ought to be very clear about the nature of the problem, and I think Kevin hit it right on the head when he said that the nature of the problem is power. After all, the Constitution is basically a power document and we sometimes tend to forget that when we debate it in the most lofty terms.

The power of television unquestionably lies in the three television networks. It seems to me we have to ask what is the nature of that power, and then, is it a healthy state of affairs for the networks to have it? In my view, that power can be described very simply as the power to exclude. The television networks put on a very homogeneous kind of programming, both in their entertainment and in their news. It is kind of shmoo-like in character, so it's very hard to get hold of it or define it. It doesn't offend any one group of our very diverse population terribly, and yet when you look at it, you notice mainly that it is exclusive—it excludes this, it excludes that, it excludes in many ways the great richness and diversity of American life and American political thought. So, the power to exclude in programming, be it entertainment or news, is a very important part of the networks' power.

The other aspect of the power to exclude is the power of the television networks and the broadcasting industry to exclude competition. Anyone who believes the television networks really don't like regulation is being very naive. The current game in Washington is that of the FCC and the Congress protecting the television broadcasters and the television networks from any meaningful economic competition so that the profits continue to roll in, and, at the same time, applying to them certain kinds of controls over programming in exchange for this protection. It's that protection from competition and the consequent exclusion of diversity of views that I think has to be recognized as the big problem in television power today.

MR. ABEL: I take it the discussion till now has not produced any outright advocacy of abolishing the FCC or regulation, although Bill Monroe went—

MR. MONROE: I'm pretty close to that.

MR. WINTER: I thought I was there.

MR. ABEL: Well, up to a point. But what Tom Whitehead is saying, what Kevin has said, seems to me to suggest that they want more regulation.

MR. PHILLIPS: More regulation of some varieties perhaps, less of others. I'm not an expert on either the regulations or the enabling statutes of the FCC. But I certainly would think that one point that deserves very minor elaboration here is the reversal of roles of the ideologies. I think of myself in this particular context as a conservative-populist—populist in the sense of opposing the new power centers. And if that is considered nonconservative by the powers that be who want to conserve those power centers, I think that it's amusing, and that it's a reversal of roles that deserves elaboration. After having seen conservatism on the losing side for a long time along with banks and railroads, I'll be happy to see it on the winning side.

MR. MONROE: I think Mr. Phillips is opposing the so-called new power centers with the theory, which Mr. Winter has commented on, of taking some power away from the networks and giving it to the federal government, which is the only way you can lessen network power through a regulatory process. This seems to me to be a remarkable thing for a conservative or a libertarian to be advocating. There is no way to cut down the power of any medium except by government supervision. And any time you do this, you enhance the government's power to, first, influence and, perhaps later, control the media. Now, if the government cannot control the sources of news in this country, we will not become an authoritarian state. But it seems to me that by enhancing the regulatory apparatus and giving the government greater leverage, greater control over the media, we would be going in that direction.

I'd like to suggest also that if we think we can get along in this country with just a genuinely free press, if we believe that newspapers can be free but broadcasting doesn't have to be, which is where we are right now, I think we're sadly mistaken, because we are developing a philosophy to the effect that government regulation can make the media perform better. We're beginning to accept that philosophy because we're accustomed to it as applied to broadcasting. And it seems to me to be a dangerous philosophy.

It's a philosophy that some students—according to one poll that came out of the University of Texas—seem to be adopting. Somebody asked a number of people in the community whether there should be a law against slanting the news. Teachers, people in the street, people in general agreed with this idea in different percentages. But the students at the university were highest of all among the categories that said, Yes, there should be a law against slanting the news. Now, this indicates a lack of perception of what the First Amendment is all about. Eventually, if we keep fastening the apparatus of regulation on broadcasting and accept this philosophy that the government can supervise the media, the newspapers are going to go down the drain as a genuinely free institution.

MR. WHITEHEAD: I have to demur slightly from your statement, Dean Abel, about my point of view and disagree almost completely with Bill. I think the premise that the only way to cut down on the power of certain institutions is to build up government power is fundamentally wrong. And yet, that's exactly what we've done in the case of television. In the 1934 Communications Act and the subsequent rules and regulations of the FCC, the government has fostered a great amount of economic, and consequently political, power in the three television networks. And then, in order to counteract that tremendous private power that it has allowed to accumulate in three hands, the government is increasing its own power. So, you have these two huge power centers, one in Washington and one in New York, trying to keep each other in some kind of balance. It's the poor viewers, it's the public, that gets caught in the middle there, and I think they're losing.

MR. ABEL: I know that you have long been concerned with this concentration of power and you've had time, since leaving the White House, perhaps, to reflect on this at leisure. How would you deal with it, without building up government power even further?

MR. WHITEHEAD: Well, I would start from the premise that both Bill and Professor Winter start with—that the First Amendment, in the kind of society we have or want to have, has to apply fully and completely to broadcasting. Broadcasting, television, the electronic media have to be full-fledged members of the press in this country. They can't be second-class citizens; they cannot be regulated by the government for the reason that Bill is talking about: the politicians and the network types interact with one another and develop a synergistic relationship that's fundamentally very unhealthy for the democratic process.

It seems to me what we have to do is to set up conditions that encourage more competition. We have to recognize that the networks can't have it both ways: they can't have their tremendous monopoly power economically *and* still have absolute freedom. This society is just not structured to allow any institution to have total freedom *and* lots of power. So, we have to look at issues of media concentration and fairness in the context of economic competition.

I agree with Bill that the fairness doctrine ought to be done away with. It's fundamentally unconstitutional. However, the only way we can justify doing away with the fairness doctrine, given the networks' economic power, is to require that the networks be prepared to sell time to anyone who wants to buy it for any kind of political broadcast so that they do not have the power they now have to decide who has access to the television medium. What the networks would like to have is for us, under the banner of the First Amendment, to do away with the fairness doctrine and then allow them to continue to have the power to refuse to sell time to people like Jack Anderson or to Mobil Oil Corp. or to any other group that they think is putting on a political message. I think that's wrong.

MR. PHILLIPS: Let me try an approach here. I think what we're dealing with is an old progression of arguments and problems that has been seen in other industries. The first and most desirable answer in any field has always been competition, the application of Jeffersonian precepts. The second and less desirable, but often necessary, answer is what I would call Rooseveltism: in other words, when an industry can't be competitive, or when there are bastions of privilege that can't be turned around by Jeffersonian processes, as in the 1930s, we have to have regulation.

In hearing Bill describe the imminent fascist peril of regulation, I was reminded of all the Wall Street lawyers that were trundled down to Washington during the mid-1930s to talk about how this or that New Deal measure would lead inevitably to Mussolini on the Potomac and that sort of thing. I think if we can't solve the problem of concentrated power in the Jeffersonian way—and I don't think we can because the power of big broadcasting will be applied to block it, just as the power of Big X or Big Y was applied in previous decades to block the remedies you're talking about—then I think, unfortunately, it's going to be necessary to have regulation to prevent the type of abusive power which the networks would like to have. They'd love to have no fairness doctrine and just sit up there and do more of what they do now.

MR. WINTER: Well, Kevin, not only do I want to disagree with you, but also I want to correct your history a little bit. The history of the New Deal is essentially a history of government and industry moving together toward monopoly. Now, if that is supposed to be reforming the concentration of power, we are a lot closer to 1984—and we were then—than we think we are. It's just utterly wrong to view the 1930s and New Deal legislation like the NRA and everything else that was done then as in any way directed towards the decentralization of power in this country. Indeed, they had specific provisos in all those laws saying that the antitrust laws did not apply.

Both you and Mr. Whitehead are talking about a problem of power which the government has created and you are providing remedies which call for more government intervention. That won't work, it simply can't work, because it creates more power rather than less, more monopoly rather than less. Any regulation of program content will be regulation designed to put in programs what the regulators want to see.

We have had in recent years a well-publicized commissioner of the FCC, well-known for thinking that licenses should be taken away because not enough "public interest programs" were being broadcast by the licensee, who, at the same time, would raise the First Amendment when the FCC cracked down on the "topless" radio broadcast. Now, that may be good taste but, as they say in the tuna ad, it doesn't taste good because it is nothing but the subjective view of that particular regulator. When a regulator is given that kind of power, power is not being decentralized, it is not being given to the average citizen of the United States; none of those things is being achieved.

MR. PHILLIPS: If I may jump in there—and incidentally I didn't suggest or even mention the NRA—if you take the Glass-Steagall Act that forced commercial banking to separate itself from investment banking, you have the type of situation that might present an analogy here. If you take extreme program control away from these people, if you take away their right to reject, as a matter of policy, any documentary made independently and to run only their own, produced in-house—that's the sort of problem we had when the banks and the investment houses were under the same roof.

MR. WINTER: Would you do that to the newspapers?

MR. PHILLIPS: Yes. I would knock cross-ownership prohibition up a couple of notches, I think.

MR. WINTER: Would you do it to the *New Republic*? Would you say you can't have a magazine like the *New Republic* without somebody being able to walk in and say:

"Here's an article I want you to print this week. It states a point of view that you never represent. Let me have access to your pages."

MR. PHILLIPS: Well, the banks have to be licensed by regulatory authorities in Washington and in their states. In the case of the broadcasters, I think there is something of a parallel in terms of the regulatory jurisdiction, which I don't regard as ephemeral, in terms of the regulatory power of the people over the airwaves.

MR. WINTER: You haven't stopped me fearing a Mussolini on the Potomac.

MR. WHITEHEAD: I have to defend myself here a little bit. While I agree with Kevin's definition of the problem, I don't want you to go away, Professor Winter, thinking that I agree with the presumption that there should be more government regulation to cure the problem, because I agree completely with you that more government regulation just exacerbates the problem.

MR. ABEL: How, then, do we deal with it?

MR. WHITEHEAD: There is ample evidence in the case of any regulated industry—be it trucking or banking or anything else—to show that the federal government is worse than private enterprise in delivering any of the kinds of services that the marketplace will sustain. And that applies, clearly, to television broadcasting. The problem, however, is that we have a very long history—some forty years now—of the courts interpreting the First Amendment of the Constitution around the framework of industry practice and FCC regulation established by the 1934 Communications Act. The courts have allowed the FCC—as they have all the other regulatory agencies set up under the New Deal—an incredible amount of discretionary power to shape broadcast industry structure and practice; they then interpret the First Amendment to fit that structure rather than ordering the FCC to change the regulatory framework to permit the First Amendment to operate unfettered. The result is that we have the FCC deciding, practically day by day, what programming is in the public interest, what is good or bad for the American people to see or hear on T.V.—a role for the federal government that is unthinkable for any other communications medium.

The broadcasters, the executives—I'm talking about the people who own and manage the networks, not those who put the programs on—are very clear as to who is important to them in terms of maintaining profit. It's the FCC. The network puts on the kind of programming that the FCC wants so that it can be sure to keep its license, so it will be immune from challenge, so it will be immune from competition, so its profits will stay high. We cannot ignore that whole history.

I agree that we should have a total hands-off policy on the part of the federal government. But we can't just change it overnight. We have to ask: how do we get from here to there?

MR. ABEL: That's exactly what I'm trying to ask.

MR. WHITEHEAD: I think that the way to get from here to there is to begin to move toward government controls that are more structurally oriented rather than end-product oriented. Today, the FCC decides, case-by-case and program-by-program, whether a program has been fair; it determines what fourteen or fifteen or sixteen program categories are good for the American people and requires broadcasters to put them on. Instead of that, we should move to something that disengages the government and yet requires the networks and broadcasters to be more responsive to that great diversity out there.

For example, the matter of access. Jack Anderson and people like that want to put on programs; other people want to buy time to express their point of view. But they can't set up a radio station or a television station even if they could afford it, because of the way we have structured the giving of licenses by the government.

So it seems to me only reasonable to approximate the conditions of a free market, in the short run at least, by saying that the people who have the monopoly right to own and operate those stations have to be willing to sell time to anyone who wants it, so that anyone who wants access can get it. That would be a step in the right direction. It wouldn't take us all the way, but it would be a start.

MR. ABEL: One objection is that it seems to reserve time for those who have the most money. There may be perfectly respectable points of view that can't command the critical mass of money.

MR. WHITEHEAD: But many of the complaints have not been from the people with lots of money; they've been from people such as Senator McGovern, who wanted to use television to reach all those people out there, so that he *could* raise money.

MR. ABEL: Bill Monroe?

MR. MONROE: May I suggest a different kind of access from that advocated by Tom Whitehead?

I'm not satisfied that television and radio, on the station level or on the network level, provide adequate access. I think there ought to be a forum in the broadcast media comparable to the letters-to-the-editor column in almost every American newspaper. A person ought to be able to write in to a station and say, "What you reported Thursday night was wrong and here's why," and have a good chance —you can't guarantee this kind of thing and it's not guaranteed in the newspapers—of having the letter published in a television form, maybe by interview. It could be worked out, I think, if broadcasting became interested enough in it.

But there is no reason why the networks should be compelled to provide the views of Jack Anderson to the country. And we are not denying the country the views of President Ford, on whose coattails Mr. Anderson sought national television exposure. So I don't think the networks are necessarily to be terribly faulted for that.

Tom, I think you were exaggerating the problem of the networks' power. The networks do have power, and examination of that power is a valid endeavor. Everybody ought to be aware of it. But the networks don't have quite the power some people think they have. You used your two fists a little while ago to emphasize that here are the networks and here is the national government. I think it was David Brinkley who raised the question: is our democracy going to be overthrown some day by CBS, or is it more likely to be overthrown by somebody in the White House?

Another thing about network power is that more of the people in the country who get their news from television get it from local stations than from the network programs. And the networks have to compete with newspapers and magazines, as well as with radio, local and network. The power of the networks is not as all-encompassing as you can easily make it seem to be.

Moreover, there is diversity among the networks. Witness the Vietnam War coverage back some years ago, where a lot of critics of television perceived a difference in approach between the ABC newscasts on the one hand, and the NBC and CBS newscasts on the other. Whether that difference existed or not, a lot of people thought it did.

MR. WHITEHEAD: I certainly wouldn't want to claim that the networks are all bad. Like any institution that makes the kind of profits they do, they must be doing something right. But, on the other hand, I can't quite accept the argument that because they do some good things they should enjoy the kind of special protection from competition that they have. I think they should have some obligations to the marketplace as well as profit from it.

The fact that I can buy a full-page or a half-page ad in the *New York Times* or in *Time* magazine or in the *New Republic* says something about the character of the print media that's missing on television. Why can't I buy five minutes of time on CBS to express my intensely held views about something? Why can't somebody out there in Keokuk, Iowa, buy five minutes of time on the local stations to get across his point of view? Why is the American public to be protected from this kind of rich diversity and confined to the very narrow kind of national viewpoint that the three networks decide to give to them? Surely the networks could schedule and profit from that kind of advertising just as they do with all the commercial ads they carry. I don't understand why there is a need for the networks to be protected to the degree that they possess that kind of power.

MR. ABEL: In fairness, I wonder whether the FCC, over a period of years, may not have made the networks much more reluctant than they might otherwise have been to provide air time for the spokesmen of unusual points of view—because they might then be required to provide time to reply, and all the rest of it, under the application of various FCC rules.

MR. WHITEHEAD: In fairness to the networks, that is definitely the case. The FCC has set up a scheme whereby the networks are held responsible for everything they put on. A requirement that they not discriminate in selling time for presenting points of view on controversial issues should be coupled with removal of the fairness doctrine for such presentations.

MR. WINTER: Isn't there a practical objection to that? Just imagine what would happen if everyone could buy five minutes of time on NBC. The networks would soon work it out, one way or another, so that all these five-minute slots were bunched at a particular time, because they wouldn't want to have the competition that would occur when everyone turned from the five minutes that was—

MR. ABEL: The rating company.

MR. MONROE: Possibly 6:00 a.m. Sunday morning.

MR. WINTER: Yes. I would think that that kind of a proposal would die of its own weight if it were put into effect. I know you favor that rather than what I was pushing because you think your proposal is more politically possible than mine. But I think if we really give any attention to it, we will find it's not. The networks, being national organizations, really have to be the way they are. You don't find McDonald's varying their hamburgers between Philadelphia and Washington. Part of their appeal is that they sell a homogeneous product; they provide advertising for Kojak or whatever all over the nation.

The networks are always going to behave in keeping with what they are. The only way around the problem, I would think, is to set up more local stations—independent stations—to make it cheaper for people to enter the broadcasting business and then see what the workings of the market bring in terms of people buying time, and the like. I'm sure any proposal allowing anyone to buy five minutes of time would, if it were in effect for a year, be laughed out of existence.

MR. ABEL: We've spent a lot of time here discussing remedies, and perhaps not enough on why remedies may be required. We've heard a lot about the homogenization of the product—which, incidentally, is a very American standard in other industries and, I guess, the secret of successful mass production. But what about the question—I think Kevin has raised it more than once in his writings—of media balance and fairness? I don't think this discussion would be complete without hearing from you about that.

MR. PHILLIPS: Well, I think there is a political element which we have to put in the equation. When talking about remedies, it's all very well to indulge in academic theory, but the fellow in Wichita or Boise or South Brooklyn doesn't want academic theory; he wants something that goes to what he's concerned about—bias, power, and so forth. And the people that will write the remedies are people in Congress and in the administration who, again, relate to a political reality syndrome. I've felt that a fair amount of this discussion here does not.

Any reasonable remedy that might be imposed in this case would have to go through the Congress of the United States—which is obviously not a highly academically oriented institution, to say the least—as well as through the communications subcommittees, which are run by people who, while not in bed with the broadcasting industry, are at least aware of the color of the covers. And I think it's a real problem—the chances are slim of getting a remedy that isn't just something basically simple that the fellow out in Main Street wants in order to put broadcasters under the thumb a little bit. When we talk about regulation we mean, basically, legislation that comes from Congress. It doesn't come from a fairy godmother who gets it out of a quarterly review, for pete's sake.

So we're talking about the regulatory process, the legislative regulatory process or the agency regulatory process. It has to be dealt with politically. It's going to come from political demands. I've seen polls; the public feels strongly about this for reasons that we all know; we've all emphasized different reasons for its concern, whether it be the McDonald's-style programming, or the power of the media, or the alleged bias. And I think this is what people should be concerned about: what the average guy in the country thinks, and wants, out of so powerful a communications network, is that he should have a say in what it does.

MR. ABEL: Anyone want to take that on?

MR. WINTER: Well, it seems to me that all regulation of program content will totally ignore the fellow in Wichita.

MR. ABEL: I think, beyond that, the uniformity, the blandness, the homogeneity—all are part of an intellectual's perception of what's wrong with American broadcasting. I'm not persuaded that most American viewers are unhappy with what they get; they like McDonald's hamburgers.

MR. PHILLIPS: I think that's quite right. Shows get ratings because people like them, some of them anyway.

MR. ABEL: Now, we may sit up here and say that people ought to prefer something else, or that their tastes are not sufficiently elevated. But what we're really talking about, it seems to me, or what Tom Whitehead seems to be talking about when he discussed access for different kinds of programs and different kinds of ideas, is the need for recognizing something the British recognized a long time ago: that there is a broad mass audience, but that there are also specialized audiences. Perhaps—as in Britain—there ought to be two separate networks: one dealing with highly specialized cultural programs and sports programs and the kinds of things for which there is a series of minority publics, obviously intersecting, and the other, like BBC-1, which, at least in my day, offered a broad-spectrum, reasonably bland product which involved, incidentally, a lot of imported American situation comedies and westerns.

MR. PHILLIPS: I think that has some appeal, but I think another possible ingredient could be included. In Germany, as I understand it, there are two television networks: one is basically oriented towards the Social Democrats and one towards the CDU. It would be very interesting to see a situation in the United States where you had one network that clearly articulated the views of the people on one side, and another that articulated the views of the people on the other side, instead of this balancing act and fairness amalgam, with snide little innuendoes about people of every persuasion slipped in when there's the chance.

MR. ABEL: Knowing a little bit about the German situation, I don't quite recognize it from your description. The so-called German networks are, in fact, a chain of regional stations—

MR. PHILLIPS: Right.

MR. ABEL: —with very large public boards. And, while there is no doubt that election returns are reflected in the appointments to the boards, the election returns have not been all that uniform, and you do find shifts in control between the SPD, the Socialist party faction, and the CDU, the Catholic party faction.

MR. MONROE: Let me point out that television, in particular—but even all of broadcasting, including radio—is a fairly new institution, as American institutions go, and institutions have a tendency to grow slowly. I've been fascinated with the way television has gradually added a lot of the specialized services provided by newspapers. The first television newscast was a newscast with a few sports scores thrown in. Later, a specialized sports reporter was added, and the specialists in other areas as well. There are now signs that the T.V. news organizations are beginning to perceive the need for something like letters to the editor; John Chancellor's "Editor's Notebook" is an example. It may not be adequate, but it's a beginning, as is the slight bow to having letters on the "60 Minutes" program. These were not present four or five years ago. I think the networks and local stations may be beginning to perceive a need for access and to provide it on a voluntary basis.

I have to enter an objection—it may be irrelevant, in a way—to Tom Whitehead's talking about the need for more competition among the networks, when he was a party, as a member of the Nixon administration, to strangling an effort by the public television network, back a few years ago, to become a genuinely competitive viable national network that would have made a fourth network in this country. And, out of ideology or whatever, the Nixon White House decided it didn't want a fourth network. It would rather have a bunch of local stations that could hardly get together on any national programming.

MR. WHITEHEAD: In response, I will only refer you to the Carnegie Report and to the legislation, which was all passed during the time of President Johnson, which is a very clear statement on the part of the Congress of the United States—not the Nixon White House—that the public television system in this country is not to become a network. It is against the law for them to become a network in the sense that you're talking about. That was not the vision that President Johnson and the liberal Congress in 1967 had in mind, and we were simply seeking to comply with the law.

Coming back, though—and I think this discussion of public television might be a good place for this—one of the big problems of television today is that it gives us *only* the Big Mac or the Quarter Pounder. It's only what McDonald's wants us to have, because that's what they do well.

And yet if you go out, you discover, in looking through the Yellow Pages, that there are an awful lot of specialized restaurants—ethnic restaurants, neighborhood restaurants —to choose from. You don't read about them all in the newspapers all the time, they don't advertise on network T.V., but they're there, and they're supported by customers.

I'm not the least bit concerned about the competition among the three television networks—or you can include public television and call it four-way competition, if you'd like. What I'm concerned about is that there is no opportunity for others to enter and compete, to set up fifth and sixth and tenth and hundredth television networks, so that all of that diversity of demand out there might be satisfied.

There has to be some way of getting television to serve all of those different interests and tastes and needs. And the way is to create opportunities for more people to come in. Now, it can be done through the federal government—which is what Kevin is saying. Kevin is perfectly right in saying the people out there are dissatisfied with the power of big institutions and want to do something about it. But if it is done through the power of big government, the media will be more and more constricted.

It seems to me that what we've got to do with television is open it up. And I, for one, don't think that there's any way, in the longer run, that we can do that effectively under the system we have. The only hope for us, it seems to me, in the longer run—and, for my part, I've only been talking about the next decade or so—is cable television. There must be enough outlets, enough channels—20, 30, 50, or 100 channels—so that all of that diversity can come out, so that people can pay directly for their own programs, instead of having to wait for 11 million other people some advertiser wants to appeal to so that it pays the networks to carry the programs. That's the ultimate answer.

MR. ABEL: Tom Whitehead, I knew we'd get around to cable eventually. I've been hearing about the promise of cable for as many years as I've been involved in broadcasting, and that goes back to 1961 or '62, and I've never seen it mature. There's something wrong with the vision of bountiful programming by talented people through a technology that seems to lack economic underpinning.

I live in New York. I see what passes for production on the cable systems. It's shoddy. It's shameful. It shouldn't be allowed. They wonder why they can't get any more subscribers. I'll tell you why: they don't provide a program service. And yet all the behavioral scientists at all the universities keep talking about the promise and the beauty of cable.

Now, how about this notion that cable television has been oversold in recent years? Does anyone have a thought about that, or am I dead wrong?

MR. WHITEHEAD: I think that many media are oversold in their early days. Your comments about cable television programming remind me a lot of what people had to say about television programming itself in the late 1940s and the early 1950s: that this was surely a trivial medium, that all the stuff it was putting on was garbage and no one should bother to take it seriously.

MR. ABEL: I think some people are saying that tonight about present-day television.

MR. WHITEHEAD: I think they are. But any new technology, be it television, radio, stereophonic records, or cable television, goes through a kind of a growth curve, and at some time it reaches the point where a critical mass of people support it and the entrepreneurs who want to provide programming begin to make a profit.

Cable, in spite of the bad press reports in the last few years, has been growing at a very steady rate, with more and more new customers and programming entrepreneurs. I think it is only a question of time until cable matures to the point where it offers the potential for the electronic media—television—to be much like the totality of the print media. You know, there is more to the print media than newspapers. There are all of those magazines out there, and I think we can hope one day that we'll have electronic magazines equivalent to our print magazines.

MR. ABEL: Now, in the second half of our discussion of the regulation of the broadcast media, we invite questions from our audience. The first question, please.

MARLENE DAVID, Washington attorney: Mr. Monroe, I share your anxiety about suppressive regulations. However, what do you do about serious instances of bias—for example, that which was supposedly revealed in a recent study about CBS misleading the American public as to the relative military strength of the United States and Soviet Russia?

MR. MONROE: Well, democracy is often a ragged process and must necessarily be so—all the loose ends cannot be tucked up. That is the weak point of my system, but I would put up with this weak point. I am not conceding the bias in the CBS program you are talking about. I don't happen to have seen the program or studied the transcript, but your version is that it was biased. That's conceivable. That's possible. I've seen some biased network programs. Networks do produce biased programs, at least occasionally. But you put up with them. You answer them as best you can by writing to the *Washington Post*, since you can't get a letter published by CBS, which I think is a mistake.

But I don't think the other option of having the government try to force fairness would work. It would put the networks or the local stations under the thumb of government to an extent that they would feel hassled by government and would frequently avoid controversial material so as not to get in trouble with government. You put up with some bias for the sake of getting a free kind of journalism which, in general, gives you a better result, better information, less government influence than you would have otherwise.

NICHOLAS JOHNSON, *Access* magazine and the National Citizens Communications Lobby: My question goes especially to Professor Winter, I believe, although I'd be interested in the others' answers, too. We're interested in answers. We want to know what we can do to provide more access and make the system work better.

I want to know what you are prepared to be for, now that I understand so clearly what it is you are against. Would you support doing something to remove the barriers to entry that AT&T and the networks have created to prevent new networks from being established? Would you require lower power for stations so that there could be more than a handful in a large community? Would you require the sale of time, for example, to the fourteen senators who requested time to answer President Nixon and were turned down by every network? Though the networks had provided the President free time, they refused to provide the United States Congress time for pay.

Would you forbid joint ownership of stations in the same community, so that there could be more owners? Would you stifle or encourage the development of cable television and pay? Would you require cable television to make channels available to all users and create sufficient channels so that that would be possible? Would you make free time available to candidates and community groups, and so on? The others have come forward with some proposals—even Bill Monroe with his idea of letters to the editor. What are yours?

MR. WINTER: For a minute I thought you wanted an answer that went something like "yes, no, yes, yes, yes, no, maybe, and I hadn't thought about it." [Laughter.] You'll forgive me if my memory misses one or two of those questions. [Laughter.]

My proposal, which I thought I had made quite clearly, was that the government ought to do the one thing which the normal operation of the market can't do, that is, to define property rights and frequencies so that people aren't broadcasting simultaneously over the same frequencies and preventing anyone from hearing anything. Having defined those, I then would make those rights subject to sale by auction by the government to anyone that wants to buy them—

MR. ABEL: Sealed bids?

MR. WINTER: Well, no, no. Sealed bids are easily rigged.

The government should auction them to anyone who wants to buy them, without requiring that they run public interest programs, handle racial matters properly, obey the fairness doctrine, give access, and all of that. These rights then could be freely exchanged. I think you would find the price of radio stations and television stations plummeting, because what people are really buying now is a government monopoly, which is what makes them so damned expensive.

I think then you would create a new structure in the industry with much easier access. I would not, under any circumstances, have the government involved in what I have been calling program content, where you force a station to let someone go on the air. It seems to me any time the government makes decisions about program content it necessarily—unless it is going to let everyone have access, which would produce more chaos than letting everyone broadcast at the same time on the same frequency—the government necessarily has to make *some* decision as to what kind of ideas are within the universe of discourse and what kind are not, what kind are worth hearing and what kind are not, and those are the very decisions I don't want the government to make.

I think that's a concrete proposal. There has been no objection to it from any member of the panel other than that it can't pass Congress because the networks are against it, and perhaps many congressmen who are allied with the networks are against it. My criticism of the networks is that they are already too far in league with the government, that they are in a way supported by the government in a monopolistic venture. I would like to see that

82

ended by getting the government out, not by getting it in any further.

HARVEY SHULMAN, Media Access Project: I have only about half as many questions as the previous questioner. First, I'd like to know how seriously you can expect your audience to take this discussion when there is no one on the panel from the FCC, which is charged with administering all the laws you are talking about. There is no one here on the panel from any of the citizens' groups around the country that are attempting to get access. It seems to be a rather academic discussion, or maybe I am wrong.

Second, and maybe this reflects my bias in this regard also, do people who are listening to this really know what the fairness doctrine is all about? Do they know that all it means is that some place in a station's overall programming it's got to put on another viewpoint? Nobody has ever mentioned that.

Third, wouldn't the suggestions that have been made here—especially the professor's latest suggestion about applying the so-called free enterprise system to the sale of licenses or Mr. Whitehead's suggestion about selling access time—in effect concentrate power even more than is true now in the large power centers in the country—the labor unions, big corporations?

And last, what about the local stations around the country? No one here on the panel has addressed that question. It seems to me that the networks perhaps are doing a better job than a lot of the local stations in hiring minorities and women and in complying with the fairness doctrine. It's where there are one- or two-market stations selling out their advertising time to utility companies or local corporations, or otherwise not allowing local groups to get on, that a lot of groups wouldn't be able to obtain true access even if the network problem were solved.

If anybody here can answer any one of those four questions, I'd be gratified.

MR. PHILLIPS: Well, I'll start by saying that I think you make one fairly important point, namely, that one set of people tend to go after the liberal networks on a political basis, and often the opposite set of people go after the local stations that reflect the local conservative power structure, whether it be coal companies, utilities, or whatever. I think this is one reason, again, why you are going to be very hard put to get anything through Congress, because Congress tends to reflect both of those power structures and, I think, wants to protect both the networks and the local stations.

I think I'd agree with about three-quarters of what Mr. Johnson said, because unlike the proposals to sell time that would be bought by DuPont or the AFL-CIO, I think his proposal deals with the regulatory world as it exists today and most of the problems that have to be hit at. I wouldn't agree with all of it, but I do agree with the bulk of it.

There are contradictory political problems in all of this. There are people who favor access in one dimension and don't favor it in the other, and who want different groups to have access. That makes the whole thing a mess, which is why I think it will stagger along in a rotten way and ultimately we'll have a heavy-handed solution.

MR. ABEL: Does anyone else have a comment on these points before we move on?

MR. WHITEHEAD: Well, I'm concerned about this idea that if you allow people to buy time somehow you're giving the power over to the people that have money. One of the nice things about money is that it's fungible, its collectible, and small groups can pool their money; people who don't have a lot of money can pool their money with others in similar circumstances. You mentioned labor unions. Individual workers do not have a lot of money. They use a labor union as a way of pooling their money to express their political point of view. I dare say your group is collecting money in order to express its point of view. The difference between paid access and governmentally mandated access is simply the terms and conditions.

In the system of television regulation we have now, we're moving perilously close to access for those who have enough political clout in Washington to get it and, to my way of thinking, that interjects the government in a fundamentally unsound way. I would much rather have the kind of freedom where people can vote with their money, pool their money, collect their money, collect their efforts and their resources, and express themselves in accordance with their numbers and the intensity of their feelings. That's much healthier and much more conducive to a free democracy than their having to use their political clout with the government.

MR. WINTER: I would like to respond just for a second to the gentleman. Apart from telling him that I'm a citizens' representative and a public interest lawyer, I want to say that I am appalled that someone who, I suspect, not many months ago was going around saying it is just terrible the way the President of the United States has sat and talked with one of his principal aides about using the regulatory power of the FCC to lift the license from a company which had criticized the administration—I am appalled that a person who held that view would now stand up and say, gee, that's a good regulatory power to have around. You know, if there was a lesson in Watergate, it was that we must reduce that kind of discretionary power in this country, not increase it.

MR. ABEL: Any questions from that side of the house?

I. WILLIAM HILL, *Editor and Publisher* magazine: I have a somewhat philosophic question, Mr. Chairman, that I would like to address to each member of the panel. Technical considerations aside, I'd like to know which approach they'd prefer, deregulation of the electronic media or regulation of the newspapers.

MR. ABEL: Interesting question. Who wants to start that one? Bill Monroe?

MR. MONROE: I think it would be much better to deregulate the electronic media, and I fear that if we do not do so, we will eventually, inevitably, regulate the print media.

MR. PHILLIPS: I suppose I would say that the only way I could really answer that would be to give you a technical answer and what might be construed as double-talk. So to go to the thrust of what I think you want, I think realistically we're going to have to impose some degree of regulation on the print media. My reason would be national security. I remember when the *Washington Post* published a photograph of a document on internal security and some form of wiretapping. It was a federal document. And Barry Goldwater said that in printing it the *Post* had violated five laws; I believe it was he who made that charge. In the political atmosphere of the time, of course, you couldn't have expected a prosecution.

I do not agree with the license the press presently enjoys in this regard. So in that particular sense I would have to come down on the side of some regulation vis-a-vis the print media, rather than favor deregulation of the broadcast media, which I just don't think would be done effectively. I think the only deregulation of the broadcast media that could take place would be Proxmire's handout to big broadcasting.

MR. ABEL: Then you would simply repeal the First Amendment?

MR. PHILLIPS: No. That's your phraseology. [Laughter.] The voice of Big Media lingers on even though you're working for an eleemosynary institution. [Laughter.]

MR. MONROE: I've got to congratulate Kevin for having the courage to go where his logic leads. A great many people who would impose or keep regulation on broadcasting don't want to apply it, or try to avoid the application of the argument, to newspapers. He is consistent in his position. I think where it leads is appalling, but he's got the consistency to go there. [Laughter.]

MR. WHITEHEAD: I think a regulated press would be anathema to the democratic process as we know it in this country. I would remove the heavy hand of government from television broadcasting at the same time that we remove the monopoly advantages that the television broadcast industry now holds.

MR. ABEL: Professor Winter?

MR. WINTER: I think it is pretty clear that I agree with Monroe and Whitehead.

MR. ABEL: Next question.

HOWARD PENNIMAN, Georgetown University: Does the case for deregulation go so far as to suggest that the broadcasters would be allowed to not broadcast any news at all or any kind of educational programs at all? I ask the question in part because I'm not sure what the answer is. There is a study that will be published soon which, among other things, seems to suggest something like the following: people who follow the news only in the print media are the least alienated, the best informed, and the least likely to be opposed to all aspects of government. Those who are most dependent upon the T.V., the inadvertent listeners—that is, the people who are being taken from the 5:00 show to the 7:30 show by means of the news media—are the ones who are most likely to dislike Congress, most likely to dislike the President, most likely to dislike business, most likely to dislike education, and most likely to like George Wallace.

I'm not suggesting anything good or bad about either of these groups, but I would like to raise a question about the kind of regulation or lack of regulation one might have.

MR. ABEL: Is that question directed to a particular member of the panel?

MR. PENNIMAN: Please start with Ralph Winter.

MR. WINTER: Well, I'm not sure I got the entire thrust, Howard. It seems to me you don't want a rule that says you can't comment on public affairs. That strikes me as a—

MR. PENNIMAN: No, what I was saying was: would

broadcasters be free, if they wished to do so, to not have news programs but simply to do other kinds of programs?

MR. ABEL: If you abolish regulation totally.

MR. WINTER: Yes, if you abolish regulation totally, by definition they would be free to do that. I want to say that it is regulation, I think, that diminishes the amount of controversial material with which television will deal, because if you know that by putting on one program you may face a big law suit with all of the attendant costs and then have to go through the cost of putting on yet another program, the logical choice is to not put on the first program.

The same thing is true with the access laws for newspapers. The reason the courts struck them down was that they thought newspapers would be less robust, less uninhibited in debate and in their editorial policy, if they were forced to permit people, at will, to reply to these things. I think there's a logic there. We live in an egalitarian age and there is a lot of egalitarian rhetoric around. There is only one condition that equalizes political communication and communication on public issues—just one condition that equalizes it for everybody—and that's silence.

MR. PHILLIPS: I think a point was made here about the Wallace supporters. They probably are the most desirous of regulation. But the principal reason that they watch television is that they are low income: it's a low-income denominator. That's where you get your highest degree of T.V. viewing. And I'm not certain that the one flows from the other. I think that low-income people tend to favor regulation of a lot of different things in this particular regard, whether it be television or oil companies or what have you. It is an economic attitude.

MR. PENNIMAN: It is across the board, Kevin, without regard to income. Whether the heavy T.V. viewers are high or low income, they are likely to be alienated. It seems to flow.

MR. WHITEHEAD: Well, I think I can answer your question very directly, because the only way to deregulate is to allow freedom. The converse of regulation is freedom. And while a rather particular problem arises now with the limited number of frequencies and so forth in broadcasting, under a somewhat deregulated broadcast system or a cable television system, where there is no need for content regulation, freedom not to do various things has to be granted. Otherwise the government would be trying to decide what is news and what is education. To me that would be a fundamental intrusion of the government over the barrier of the First Amendment.

MR. MONROE: It should be said that whereas deregulation would mean freedom for a radio station to play records all day or for a television station to show soap operas all day, there is no chance in the world that any stations to speak of would do without news, particularly television stations. News has developed in television, bit by bit, and the time devoted to it has expanded from fifteen minutes to a half hour on the network level, and from a half hour to an hour to an hour-and-a-half on many local stations, both in the morning and in the late evening, in response to need. It is important to the stations because the early evening newscasts set up an audience that goes into the evening, and because it makes a profit. I don't think we need fear deregulation on the basis that news would disappear. It would not.

MR. ABEL: A question from this side of the house.

CARL EIFERT, Senator Proxmire's staff: I would like reactions from members of the panel to a couple of observations about things that have not really been talked about tonight, although Professor Winter alluded to them in the last question. Earlier we were talking about the impossibility of buying time for various ideas, the blandness and homogeneity of programming, and that sort of thing. Homogeneity exists because of government regulation. And the only way to get diversity, it seems to me, would be to do away with government regulation, as Professor Winter said.

    Second, I haven't heard anything tonight about the

psychology of listening. Just what effect do radio and T.V., newspapers, and other media have on people? The implicit assumption always seems to be that everyone is going to go out and do what he heard on the last T.V. program. If that were true, there would be no need for a democracy, a representative republican form of government.

Another thing I didn't hear any mention of is the libel laws. The Supreme Court, in interpreting state laws— we haven't had any federal libel laws since the Alien and Sedition Acts—in libel cases, says that we have to be very careful of punishment, punitive damages, and so on, because they would lead to self-censorship. So, therefore, we have to tolerate quite a bit of lying, if you will. But on the other hand in the *Red Lion* case, the Supreme Court said the fairness doctrine enhances the First Amendment, which is basically a negative—a prohibition. You cannot enhance a negative. Negative times negative is still nothing.

And my last point goes to the very philosophy of the First Amendment, which is that there is no such thing as a right to know; last night's panel brought this out. Rather, the system is set up so that prohibiting the government from controlling what is printed and said—and a couple of other freedoms like assembly, petitioning, writing grievances, religion, and so on—amounts to a prohibition designed to guarantee freedom, and who knows what freedom is going to bring. But that's what the founders, the authors of the Constitution, brought up because they themselves were products of the age of reason.

If you would comment?

MR. ABEL: Is that a question or an observation? I am having a little difficulty getting a handle on it.

MR. EIFERT: Well, they were observations of what I thought had not been brought out tonight and I would like some reaction, if people would care to react.

MR. ABEL: Anyone care to react?

MR. PHILLIPS: To take the spirit of the First Amendment and the general concept that you are raising there, I think

90

we should remember that the First Amendment, as it was originally formulated, flowed out of essentially Anglo-Saxon law and attitudes. If we look at the rest of the English-speaking world and the legal structures that prevail today, we find government-regulated television in the United Kingdom, Australia, and Canada. Those countries have regulation and nobody's screaming that it is abrogating the rights of freeborn Englishmen.

The press is regulated in Canada and Britain. In the latter there is a substantial trial going on right now based on the powers of the government to block the publication of the sort of document that's caused so much trouble in the United States in the last two or three years. It's an obvious fact of British legal life at the present time. So I think the First Amendment should be considered in the context of where it came from, not in the context of the image that's been blazoned in the United States by the media spokesmen.

MR. MONROE: Well, I think, in terms of addressing the spirit of the First Amendment, it might be said that former Senator Sam Ervin, who is looked on as an eminent constitutional lawyer, thought that if the men who wrote the First Amendment had been aware of the technology to come, they would have specifically included radio and television along with press in the First Amendment. And his opinion was that, by function, in terms of informing the public by providing news, radio and television were doing exactly what the First Amendment was designed to protect. And there was no doubt in Senator Ervin's mind that the First Amendment would have been designed to protect these media specifically and to prevent the kind of regulation we now have, had these men been able to anticipate the technology. As Reuven Frank of NBC put it, we have a case here of the First Amendment having been repealed by technology.

I can't comment on what Mr. Eifert said, except basically to agree with it. But I'm personally grateful to Senator Proxmire for sponsoring a bill to abolish the fairness doctrine. I think it's important that this is happening. We have had some suggestion here tonight that we must not go into this remedy and that one, because maybe they are not possible politically. Well, a few years ago nobody would have anticipated that Senator Proxmire, who was involved originally in writing the fairness doctrine, if I understand correctly, would now be one of the leading advocates—perhaps *the* leading advocate—of abolishing it.

Likewise, we can figure that there is no reason why the Supreme Court may not come out with a decision—not next year or three years from now, but maybe ten years from now—that would go against *Red Lion*, because the Supreme Court is subject to change as well. As a matter of fact, in that decision and others, the Supreme Court has revealed some of the ambiguities, to say the least, of the First Amendment as it applies to broadcasting.

MR. WHITEHEAD: The trouble with the philosophy behind the First Amendment is that most people don't really understand it. There is no doubt that the United States has gone a lot farther than Britain in guaranteeing freedom. But so many people I've talked to over the years seem to think that the First Amendment says Congress shall make no law abridging the freedom of the press except for good causes.

And, of course, each of us is the keeper of good causes. Many liberals think that the freedom of the networks to do battle against the conservatives and so forth is a wonderful thing, and that the networks ought to be maintained totally free, especially in their news departments that lean toward that particular political persuasion. Other liberals think that the networks should be cut back in certain areas, that they should not be allowed to put on so many ads or so little cultural programming. Everyone seems perfectly willing to endorse the First Amendment, or exempt the First Amendment, according to where they benefit. The networks proclaim that they want the First Amendment to apply totally, and yet they hide behind it at every encounter when the FCC or the Antitrust Division or a court attempts to put on them some of the same kinds of restrictions that the rest of us and other corporations have.

I think what we have here is a fundamental question

of philosophy, Kevin. Do we *want* to be more like the British? Do we *want* to have the government intermingled with the private sector in determining what we see and hear? Or do we want the dissemination of ideas in our society to be totally outside the realm of the government? I, for one, think that the latter view is the only desirable one for this country.

MR. PHILLIPS: Well, I think it comes down to the question of whether or not you think that effective dissemination of ideas can occur without the government remedying the concentration which you would resist. I think that's one of the problems. It is not an exclusive either/or.

MR. WHITEHEAD: That's correct. The government has to be willing to remedy some of the conditions that it has created. You witness such cases even in the print media. Back in the 1940s there was the antitrust case against the Associated Press, where the Supreme Court upheld certain limitations on the print media in favor of competition and the free dissemination of ideas. I think we have to have the same kind of philosophy when it comes to the electronic media.

MR. ABEL: Let's get back to our questioners.

REED IRVINE, Accuracy in Media: I have two questions. First, in the light of all that has been said about the Founding Fathers, I wonder if any of the panelists is aware that Thomas Jefferson based his opposition to the Alien and Sedition Acts on the fact that he considered the sedition laws and the libel laws, the restrictive laws on the press of the states, to be fully adequate to the purpose, and, therefore, he didn't believe any federal law was necessary.

Second, we have been trying for some time to get the networks, NBC and others, to tell us how they feel about this situation. This is directed mainly to Mr. Monroe. Given the kind of situation that Professor Winter envisions, in which anyone can buy control, let us assume that some rich Texas oil man or Saudi sheik or someone were to buy control of all three networks, that all three fell into conservative hands. Walter Cronkite would be replaced by Paul Harvey, Eric Sevareid would be replaced by Bill Buckley, John Chancellor by Bob Hurley, and Brinkley by Jeffrey St. John, and similarly with ABC. When television reported, for example, the OAS abandoning the sanctions on Cuba, instead of having comments from Senator Kennedy and Senator Percy, we would have comments from Senator Helms and Senator Thurmond, and so on down the line. Would not the people in NBC and the liberals, who are now clamoring for abolition of the fairness doctrine, be clamoring for a restoration of the fairness doctrine, and wouldn't Professors Winter and Whitehead then be joining them—or not?

MR. MONROE: I can't speak for the networks, Mr. Irvine. I don't know what position NBC or any other network would take about this general issue. As far as I'm concerned, there's little likelihood, if any, of any network newscast being biased in a definite, clear-cut direction, with either conservative or liberal commentators giving outright conservative or liberal opinions night after night, because the competition among the networks would preclude that.

If you recall, during the Vietnam War—I alluded to this a while ago—there was a feeling that CBS and NBC were against the war. There was a particular period when some people felt the networks, these networks, were a little biased. For a while, Howard K. Smith was perceived as a hawk on Vietnam. And some people who watched ratings among the network newscasts thought that the rating of the ABC program went up a bit at this point because those who didn't like what they perceived to be the anti-Vietnam view on the Huntley-Brinkley program and on the Cronkite program went over to watch Howard K. Smith. This kind of public reaction to a perceived bias will prevent the networks from engaging in any outright bias.

MR. ABEL: Before we go on, did you have a reply to that?

MR. WINTER: Well, all I can say is that I'm in the position of being able to answer that question because I generally agree with the questioner. I think the networks do exhibit a bias. I think it's quite obvious at times. And I think that they can be very sloppy and they can be sloppy in one particular direction. So I'm in a position to say to you, even though they do go in a way that is opposite to my own views on the world, I still want to leave them free.

MR. IRVINE: Does any of you have an answer to my first question about Thomas Jefferson?

MR. MONROE: I am aware that Thomas Jefferson said that, yes. [Laughter.]

MR. ABEL: We'll go to this side of the house, here.

VERA GLASER, Knight Newspapers: The panel has barely touched on public broadcasting, and it seems to me that it might be very interesting and perhaps relevant here if we could get a quick opinion from each of the panel members as to the usefulness of public broadcasting. For example, do you think it has set an example in moving us away from some of the shortcomings that we have been talking about—bias, and so on—or has it merely turned out to be, in its short history, a carbon copy of commercial broadcasting?

MR. PHILLIPS: I'll start on that. I don't think public television has become a carbon copy of commercial television. I think it's developed a new form of obnoxiousness that doesn't reflect the pattern of commercial television.

For example, Channel 13 up in New York recently had a show where they interviewed Abbie Hoffman; they had tracked him down and paid him $2,500. Now, the networks will pay $2,500 for a hot ticket, but they will not meet with somebody who's under federal charges at the time and then let him edit the tapes and so forth, and say that this was a hot thing to put on television because there's a great public demand for it.

This reflects an attitude on the part of a lot of the public broadcasting people. They're looking for a different type of thing. I don't think they duplicate commercial television. I think that in public affairs programming they often have a kind of new-leftish tilt, which I think is rather unproductive and unfortunate. I like their dramatic, operatic, and symphonic programs. I think they're useful. I think that's all they ought to do. They ought to leave the public affairs programs to people whose range of awareness goes beyond Abbie Hoffman and insulting French people in Louisiana.

MR. WHITEHEAD: I think public television has added measurably to the coverage of the diversity that we have available to us in this country. Public T.V. largely goes after a minority audience. That's what it was originally conceived to do, to present alternatives to the mass-audience fare that the commercial networks tend to put on. And you have to give it some credit for developing some programming that we would not otherwise have available to us, for trying to offer a slightly higher cut of programming.

On the other hand, it was supposed to provide an across-the-board alternative for all of us, and there's some reason to believe that it is mainly satisfying the affluent and intellectual interest in alternatives to commercial television. You wonder where all of the other alternatives are.

MR. MONROE: I think public television could be a lively and worthwhile competitor to the commercial networks, particularly in regard to news and information. But it has been denied—primarily by the Nixon administration and to some extent by the Congress—the insulation from government that would help it, the regular funding that would help it, and the structure that would make it viable on a national basis.

MR. WHITEHEAD: I just have to point out one more time, Bill, that the Nixon administration proposed a five-year funding bill which *would* provide significant insulation from both the White House and the Congress. The Congress is refusing to pass such a bill, opting instead for one-year funding.

MR. ABEL: I happen to have some involvement with

public television, and to me it's disappointing. Television is a vastly expensive medium. I don't think the critical mass of money or of talent has ever been made available to give us a real taste of what public television is capable of. I believe this last funding bill provided $65 million; is that right?

MR. WHITEHEAD: I think the final version was $80 million going up to $100-and-some million.

MR. ABEL: No, but I mean for this next year.

MR. WHITEHEAD: I think that's right.

MR. ABEL: Now, that's $80 million to be divided among 200-odd stations. It's not a great deal of money. When you compare it with the budget of, say, a local station like WCBS in New York, it's a joke.

I am disappointed with public television. I think its triumphs, the ones that Kevin mentioned, are by and large imported triumphs. Some of them I knew well on the BBC before they ever came over here. I don't argue that they shouldn't have been brought over. But I don't have a sense that the creative excitement that I know exists in American journalism, in American theater, and in the American arts is getting through on public television. And I'm very disappointed about that.

MR. WINTER: Isn't there an issue about public television that goes beyond whether we like the programs or whether they could be improved? There is, first, the question of whether public television is the right remedy, the best remedy, for some of the evils we've all conceded exist in the present situation. Beyond that, it seems to me to be a vehicle sitting there, ready to take over the private networks.

But my understanding of what has happened in foreign countries when the government has owned the television stations is contrary to the happy view we hear. As I understand it, DeGaulle was able to keep himself on and to exclude his competitors far beyond anything that ever

97

happens in the United States. Winston Churchill, I understand, was not allowed to appear on the BBC until he returned to the cabinet in 1939, I guess, because he was thought to be too controversial.

There seem to be some very fundamental questions beyond whether the programs are good or bad, and I'm not sure that the answer cuts at all in the direction of saying that we ought to continue to support public broadcasting without really addressing those questions.

MR. ABEL: In fairness, I'd like to observe that, while it is perfectly clear that public television in France was a direct instrument of the presidency—I was there at the time of the student rioting in 1968, for example, when not a foot of film of those riots was allowed to be shown on French television on DeGaulle's personal orders—I think it would be a mistake to assume that, because that happened in France, every other form of noncommercial broadcasting in other countries is under the same arrangement. The BBC and the West German television are the ones that I know best, and I would argue that there is at least as great a diversity of viewpoint on those noncommercial systems as we have in the United States, in total. That's my personal view.

OWEN FRISBY, Chase Manhattan Bank: I'd like to ask Kevin Phillips to comment on something that two of the other panelists commented on a minute ago. There are hundreds of newspapers with varying philosophical points of view in their editorial pages and hundreds of columnists, ranging from liberals to conservatives, who present an equally wide variety of opinion in the print media. Now, how would you characterize the philosophical balance and make-up of not only the anchormen but the principal on-camera newsmen on the three networks, from the standpoint of philosophical balance on the major issues of the day?

MR. PHILLIPS: Well, my own characterization would be too subjective, so I'll cite that of a poll of which I have some knowledge and with which I have been somewhat associated—so I have to say there's a minor subjective element in there, perhaps. But the people polled generally perceive Walter Cronkite, Dan Rather, and other people that have been attacked and identified as liberals, as liberals, and think of them, to that extent, as biased. John Chancellor came out quite well in this particular poll. People saw him as in the middle, pretty much down the line. And Howard K. Smith and Harry Reasoner came out as moderates, sometimes moderate conservatives.

A minority felt that the networks' coverage of the major issues was biased in the liberal direction. Another minority felt that there wasn't any real bias. Hardly anybody felt that network coverage was biased towards the conservative view. You get that only among New Left types who think that everybody to the right of Ron Dellums is a part of the establishment or something. So, I dismiss the idea that the great bulk of the country thinks that there's a conservative slant to network news; I think it's divided between those who think the news is sort of where it ought to be and those that think it's too liberal.

BILL OLSON, law student, University of Richmond: My question is for Mr. Monroe. Earlier this evening, you praised Mr. Phillips for his consistency, even though you didn't agree with him, and I'd like to give you an opportunity to be consistent yourself on one point.

You advocate getting the government out of programming, particularly abolishing the fairness doctrine. My question is whether or not you would agree with the suggestion made by Professor Winter and Mr. Whitehead concerning the selling off of the airwaves, or do you advocate only selective deregulation? The question is, do you only believe in freedom and competition where they help and not where they hurt, or are you willing to take the burdens as well as the benefits?

MR. MONROE: There may be several ways of going about arranging a system where a license gives you freedom to operate. Mr. Winter's way is one possibility. I think it's an interesting possibility. I think if we did what he suggests, we'd be better off than we are now, because the broadcast media would have, as I believe he said, an equivalent freedom to what the newspapers have. And it's almost impossible to arrange a system where broadcasters are literally as free as newspaper publishers, unless you go to something like licenses in perpetuity.

If you're going to do that, you need to distribute the channels one way or another. Mr. Winter is not the first to suggest a sort of auction. That would be one way of doing it. The way it is done is not as important to me as getting to a system where a license means, as long as you stay on your channel, the FCC will be simply a technical monitor. You can operate with the same freedom and lack of worry about pressure from government as newspaper people do.

So, in a sense, I am in agreement with Mr. Winter. I'm not sure that's the only way to do it, but I think it's a good system in comparison with what we now have. Now, this is not my network's position, I don't think.

MR. ABEL: I think there's time for one more question before we adjourn.

JIM HINISH, legislative assistant to Senator Fannin: I'd like to ask these gentlemen: in addition to favoring deregulation, would you also favor a vigorous antitrust policy to get at the problem of concentration of power that has been posed by Mr. Phillips?

MR. WHITEHEAD: You can't have one without the other.

MR. ABEL: I'm not sure the audience completely caught what you're saying. Would you expand slightly?

MR. WHITEHEAD: I'm saying you cannot have deregulation of the kind of network power that is now being held in check by the federal government—you can't remove that federal power—unless the networks are more answerable to the competition in the marketplace. And no company that I've ever heard of in any line of business responds to competition unless it's made to, that is, through the antitrust laws.

MR. ABEL: The answer, then, is yes?

MR. WHITEHEAD: Yes.

MR. ABEL: In closing, I want to thank our panelists: Bill Monroe of NBC news; Kevin Phillips, author and syndicated columnist; Clay Whitehead, former director of the U.S. Office of Telecommunications; and Professor Ralph Winter of the Yale Law School. And thank you all for being with us. Good night. [Applause.]